THE PROGRESSIONS OF
CLASSICAL BALLET TECHNIQUE

ROYAL ACADEMY OF
DANCE

THE PROGRESSIONS OF CLASSICAL BALLET TECHNIQUE

DEDICATION

This book is dedicated to the memory of Philip Richardson OBE (1875-1963). Philip Richardson was the founding editor of *Dancing Times* and a founder member of the Association of Teachers of Operatic Dancing of Great Britain, later to become the Royal Academy of Dance. Eminent dance writer and critic, collector of literature on dance from the Renaissance onward, Philip Richardson donated his collection, comprising many rare books on dance, to the Academy. Through his work with students on the Academy's Teacher Training Course, Richardson became involved in teacher education and training. The sale of part of the Philip Richardson collection has supported the production of *The Progressions of Classical Ballet Technique* which we hope will become an important resource for teachers and students of ballet throughout the world.

CONTENTS

CONTENTS

CONTENTS

CONTENTS

CONTENTS

FOREWORD
BY DAME ANTOINETTE SIBLEY DBE

It is very exciting that Lynn Wallis, Artistic Director of the Royal Academy of Dance, and her eminent panel have written a follow-up to *The Foundations of Classical Ballet Technique*. *Foundations* deals with the purely basic steps – defining what these basic positions and movements are, why they are important, and how they should be performed.

The Progressions of Classical Ballet Technique, as its title implies, moves on. It is intended for a higher level of student altogether and, in fact, should only be used by the more advanced student. This book picks up where the first left off, so where, for example, you would find a single pirouette in the first book, this develops into a double pirouette, an embellished pirouette, or a more complex turn like fouetté rond de jambe en tournant. Students now start to learn all the glorious, fun steps – this is really dancing: sauts de basque, gargouillades, temps de poisson, renversés, flic-flacs, etc. All of these steps are taken to pieces, and dissected so that the students know precisely what they are trying to achieve. Once the technique has been mastered, the students will begin to find their own way of "feeling" the steps through the movement and the music. As Tamara Karsavina once said, "Remember that the mechanism of the dance becomes artistry only when it is inspired by feeling".

The Progressions of Classical Ballet Technique is an important, invaluable book that will help and inspire every advanced teacher, examiner and student. It is a perfect companion to *The Foundations of Classical Ballet Technique*.

Dame Antoinette Sibley DBE
PRESIDENT

ARTISTIC PANEL

MORWENNA BOWEN   FRAD

Throughout her teaching career Morwenna Bowen worked with the late Phyllis Kempster, who founded a school in the Midlands area in 1945 to develop standards of excellence in classical ballet. She assisted Phyllis Kempster in the development of a Youth Ballet Company which was founded in 1975. She now continues as Principal of the school and Artistic Director of the Youth Ballet.

Morwenna has been closely associated with the Royal Academy of Dance in the development and teaching of various syllabus levels, notably as a member of the panel that created the Major Examination Syllabus and training programme that was launched in 1986. She was appointed as a Children's examiner in the early 1960s and subsequently as a Major examiner in 1969. Since 1971 she has been a member of the Executive Committee of the Academy, and is currently Chairman of the Artistic Committee. She was awarded a Fellowship in 1986. She was also a member of the artistic panel for the creation of *The Foundations of Classical Ballet Technique* published in 1997.

FRANK FREEMAN   FRAD ARAD Dip.PDTC

Frank Freeman is an international freelance teacher and choreographer, and a Vocational Graded examiner for the Royal Academy of Dance. Entirely trained at The Royal Ballet School, he graduated into the main company of The Royal Ballet at the Royal Opera House, Covent Garden. He was also a member of The Royal Ballet's educational group "Ballet For All" and later joined English National Ballet.

In 1976 Frank completed the Academy's Professional Dancer's Teaching Course graduating with distinction in all subjects. For many years he has lectured on and examined the Professional Dancer's Teaching Course and he has been regularly involved in the training of new Vocational examiners. He has taught in most of the leading vocational schools in Great Britain and he has choreographed extensively both here and abroad. He is a founder Patron of the National Youth Ballet of Great Britain.

Frank writes articles and reviews for the leading dance magazines and was a member of the artistic panel for the creation of *The Foundations of Classical Ballet Technique* published in 1997. He has been a member of the judging panel for dance for the Sir Laurence Olivier Awards and is a member of the faculty of The Royal Ballet School. In April 2000 he was awarded a Fellowship by the Royal Academy of Dance, and was co-opted onto the Academy's Artistic Committee.

MOIRA McCORMACK   MCSP ARAD Dip.PDTC

Moira McCormack graduated from The Royal Ballet School in 1973, going on to dance with Sadler's Wells Royal Ballet, National Ballet of Canada, and London Festival Ballet. An interest in teaching took her to the Professional Dancer's Teaching Course and a teaching career, but a concern about dancers' health and welfare lead her to physiotherapy training at Guy's Hospital. The relationship between teaching methods, physique, and injury is a continuing and driving interest for her.

Moira has been invited on many occasions to teach and conduct seminars internationally and regularly lectures at the Royal Academy of Dance and The Royal Ballet School. She worked as physiotherapist to The Royal Ballet School for five years and was a member of the artistic panel for the creation of *The Foundations of Classical Ballet Technique*. She is a co-opted member of the Academy's Artistic Committee and is currently Senior Physiotherapist to The Royal Ballet Company at the Royal Opera House.

ARTISTIC PANEL

RHONDA RYMAN - EDITOR MA AI CHOR FI CHOR
Rhonda Ryman is currently an Associate Professor at the University of Waterloo, Ontario, Canada, where she has taught courses including Dance Notation and Reconstruction as well as Principles of Dance Technique for over twenty-five years. Since 1995 she has been an Adjunct Professor in the Graduate Program in Dance, York University, Toronto. She is a Fellow of the International Council of Kinetography Laban and of The Benesh Institute, and has published reviews and articles in publications such as *Dance in Canada, Dance Notation Journal, Dance Research, Dance Research Journal,* and *The Choreologist.*

She has authored the two-volume *RAD Grades Examination Syllabus Recorded in Benesh Movement Notation* (London: The Benesh Institute, 1994), *Dictionary of Classical Ballet Terminology* (London: Royal Academy of Dancing, 1998), and *Ryman's Dictionary of Classical Ballet Terms: Cecchetti Method* (Toronto: Dance Collection Danse, 1998). Her recent electronic publication, *Ballet Moves* (http://www.charactermotion.com), uses Life Forms computer animation software to represent classical ballet movements and repertoire. Continuing her work as editor and member of the artistic panel for *The Foundations of Classical Ballet Technique,* she has written the introductory essays and Benesh Movement Notation for *The Progressions of Classical Ballet Technique.*

LYNN WALLIS - PANEL CHAIRMAN   FISTD
Lynn Wallis graduated from The Royal Ballet Senior School in 1965 into The Royal Ballet Touring Company, becoming Ballet Mistress at the school in 1969, a position she held until 1982, when she was made Deputy Principal. During this time she reproduced a great many ballets from the classical repertoire for the school performances at the Royal Opera House, Covent Garden, and other venues. In 1984, at the invitation of Erik Bruhn, she joined the National Ballet of Canada, as Artistic Co-ordinator, and in 1986 she became Associate Artistic Director, with Valerie Wilder, and Co-Artistic Director from 1987 to 1989. In 1990 she was appointed Deputy Artistic Director of English National Ballet with special responsibility for mid-scale touring, the Education and Community Unit, Choreographic workshop and English National Ballet School.

Lynn joined the Royal Academy of Dance in 1994 as Artistic Director and is responsible for setting and maintaining the standards of dance training world-wide, developing the Academy's syllabus and planning courses internationally for students. Lynn was appointed Honorary President of the Greek region of the RAD in June 2000. In 2001 she became Chair of the RAD's Board of Examiners. More recently, Lynn has been involved in the introduction of the new marking system and the accreditation of RAD examinations by the Qualifications and Curriculum Authority in England and its partner regulatory authorities in Wales and Northern Ireland.

Lynn was chairman of a panel of dance professionals who wrote *The Foundations of Classical Ballet Technique* and was instrumental in leading the panel in writing the sequel, *The Progressions of Classical Ballet Technique.* In 2001 she was nominated and short-listed for the European Women of Achievement Awards.

INTRODUCTION

Ideally, the goal of advanced dance study is the attainment of pure classical technique – clean, precise, and strong. To achieve this end safely, the individual dancer's physique must be studied and understood. Although the ideal form can be clearly defined and described for each position or action, every dancer finds his or her own way of embodying its essence. Dancers excel by infusing each movement with their own interpretation, rather than by imitating in a sterile and robot-like manner.

Advanced training offers great physical challenges. The dancer must possess a secure level of basic technique and proficiency in order to perform more complex movements at this level. Integral to dance training is a careful building of the strength, flexibility, and agility required to sustain the demands of advanced movements and professional choreography. While not all physiques are able to master the highest levels of dance technique, understanding and observing safe dance practice can bring great physical benefits to those pursuing it.

The following simple rules contribute to the care of the dancer's instrument. Knees and feet must be worked in alignment with correct spinal posture in order to build a balanced musculature that is stable and centred. All dance footwear should fit perfectly to allow correct weight bearing through the foot and complement the line of the leg. Floors should be well sprung for shock absorption, and their surface should offer the right amount of friction. A slippery floor will produce increased tension in the legs and an unduly sticky floor can cause joint strain. To promote good muscle function, temperatures should not drop below 20 degrees Celsius in studios and theatres. Since muscles also need constant fluid levels, dancers should drink small amounts of water between barre work and centre practice. Also, while explanation is an expected part of training, teachers should keep to a minimum the times when the dancer is static and waiting, to avoid cooling down.

Vocational studies in dance offer many challenges and rewards beyond the acquisition of ballet skills. As dancers master each level of technique, they achieve greater physical and mental confidence. They come to appreciate the strengths and limitations of their own instrument and to adopt safe dance practices as their technical repertoire expands. In addition to mastering a greater variety of movements involving co-ordination of the entire body, each dancer is challenged to understand the underlying motivation that inspires a movement and makes it uniquely expressive. Beyond physical aptitude, this requires a mature and sensitive approach to performance. The higher the level of study, the more complex are the ways in which movements are linked together, developing mental as well as physical flexibility and agility. Each phrase of movement is informed by a broader, richer awareness of the performance space, and by sensitivity to the rhythm, texture, and contour of the music. In each class, dancers learn to respond to music by conveying its dynamic values through the body, to make visible their feelings and emotions. Each class offers opportunities for personal growth and expression.

ABOUT THIS BOOK

This book is a companion volume and sequel to *The Foundations of Classical Ballet* (RAD 1997). It should be used in conjunction with the *Foundations* text and assumes a thorough theoretical and practical understanding of its contents. This includes knowledge of the elements that underpin ballet technique (e.g. posture, placement, alignment), as well as basic vocabulary (positions of the feet and arms, poses of the body, etc.). It also presupposes knowledge of the organisation and structure of a ballet class, from barre work to pointe work, and an understanding of the contents and goals of each part of the class. Explanations of concepts and movements in the *Foundations* book will therefore not be revisited in this volume. It is geared at a more advanced level of training and focuses on concepts and vocabulary relevant to dance training beyond the elementary level.

A few general comments apply throughout. Although full leg extensions are described at the classical 90 degrees, the increasing demands of contemporary dance practice often require higher extensions. It is understood that full extensions may be taken higher, according to the individual's physique and to safe dance practice. Although this book provides simple clear examples of musical accompaniment for each movement introduced, it is understood that alternative time signatures may be used, since musical accompaniment varies widely at this level.

Continuing the practice initiated in *Foundations*, Benesh Movement Notation is included to illustrate a basic example of each movement performed in an appropriate time signature. The notation shows each step performed with basic arms, alignment, and timing. These may differ slightly from the *Progressions* word descriptions which often contain explicit information assumed by convention in Benesh Movement Notation. The notated examples may also differ from the published *Vocational Graded Examination Syllabus* notation which shows choreographed sequences.

CONTENTS
CHAPTER ONE: BARRE WORK

CHAPTER ONE
BARRE WORK

In even the earliest stages of training, barre work prepares the dancer for what is to come in the centre practice and subsequent parts of each class, and ultimately for the performance of repertoire on stage. The movements selected for inclusion in this chapter are integral parts of steps that more advanced students will be dancing in the centre, often in increasingly complex forms. For example, battement glissé with battement piqué develops the speed and strength used in petit allegro jumps and beats such as cabrioles. The broader action of grand battement with battement piqué builds the lightness and leg strength needed to initiate grand allegro jumps like assemblé dessus en tournant. Battement fouetté at 45 degrees increases turnout and stability for fouetté turns as well as adage and allegro fouetté actions. Rond de jambe jeté encourages mobility and freedom in the hip socket necessary for expansive actions like grand fouetté relevé en tournant. Since the range of advanced vocabulary is so broad, it is important to design each class by selecting barre exercises that relate to movements to be performed later in the class, and to balance these over a span of classes.

At more advanced levels of training, barre movements described in *Foundations* may be taken en demi-pointe or en pointe throughout the barre work section of the class, rather than in a separate section after it. Since the mechanics of a basic rise or relevé (see *Foundations*, pages 51-52, 102-103) apply to more advanced actions, it is not necessary to restate them in reference to actions such as grand battement en demi-pointe or en pointe.

In addition to preparing specific steps, barre work warms up and strengthens the body as well as focusing the mind. It may be a little shorter at more advanced levels to conserve the dancer's energy for the increasing demands of centre enchaînements. It is also kept simple and uncluttered. The great range of vocabulary allows countless combinations and sequencing, but solid training requires care and patience. If barre work is too complex, however, the dancer concentrates on mastering the choreography rather than on understanding each component movement. In the later stages of training, movements that naturally complement each other can be combined to streamline the barre. For example, a rond de jambe à terre can be linked with a rond de jambe jeté. A well-designed barre balances complexity and elegant simplicity. Its richness derives from the way the movements are amalgamated, not in the intricacy of the choreography.

Since the range of advanced vocabulary is so broad, it is not possible to cover every step in every class. Each class must be well designed as part of an overall plan, balancing the steps to be covered in the course of a week, a month or more. The build-up over a span of classes is important.

POSITIONS OF THE ARMS

These continue from *Foundations*, page 12.

OPEN 5TH POSITION

An extended 5th position of the arms with the palms facing outward and the head and eye focus slightly raised.

Open 5th position of the arms

OPEN 4TH POSITION

An extended 4th position of the arms with the palms facing downward, creating a diagonal line from centre finger to centre finger. The head is turned toward the raised arm and the eye focus is directed over and beyond the hand, complementing the elongated line.

Open 4th position of the arms

PLACEMENTS OF THE WORKING LEG

These continue from *Foundations*, page 15.

4TH POSITION DEVANT

A position of the raised leg, fully stretched in front of the body at various heights.

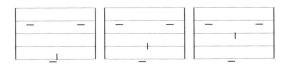

4th position devant à terre, 45 degrees, 90 degrees

4TH POSITION DERRIERE

A position of the raised leg, fully stretched behind the body at various heights.

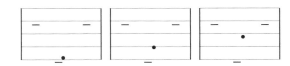

4th position derrière à terre, 45 degrees, 90 degrees

4TH POSITION EN FONDU Lunge

An extended 4th position in which the front leg is en fondu and the back leg is straight. The majority of the weight is over the front leg, and varying depths of fondu are used depending on the context of the movement. For example, a port de bras in 4th position en fondu employs a deeper fondu than a preparation for a pirouette en dedans.

4th position en fondu as in port de bras in 4th position en fondu

4th position en fondu as in preparation for pirouette en dedans

BATTEMENT GLISSE WITH BATTEMENT PIQUE

See *Foundations*, page 32.

A battement glissé incorporating a piqué action.

It is a movement to develop speed and strength.

Following the initial opening action, the working leg lowers à terre remaining fully stretched and immediately rebounds to its previous height with a quick, sharp movement, before closing to complete the battement action.

Various time signatures may be used, with the rebound action completed on the musical beat.

This movement may also be taken incorporating two piqué actions with the second rebound completed on the musical beat.

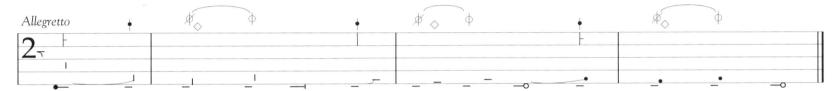

Battement glissé with battement piqué devant, to 2nd position, and derrière in 2/4 time

GRAND BATTEMENT WITH BATTEMENT PIQUE

See *Foundations*, page 49.

A grand battement incorporating a piqué action.

It is a movement to develop lightness and strength of the leg in preparation for grand allegro.

Following the initial opening action, the working leg lowers à terre remaining fully stretched and immediately rebounds to its previous height with a quick, sharp movement, before closing to complete the battement action.

Various time signatures may be used, with the rebound completed on the musical beat.

This movement may also be taken incorporating two piqué actions.

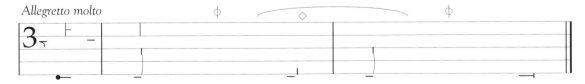

Grand battement with battement piqué devant in 3/4 time

BATTEMENT FOUETTE AT 45 DEGREES

A whipping action of the working leg at 45 degrees tracing a 90-degree arc.

This movement develops turnout and stability.

From 5th position the leg executes a battement to 4th position devant en l'air at 45 degrees and, retaining its height, makes a fouetté to 2nd position.

The movement may be taken en dehors from 4th position devant or 2nd position, or en dedans from 4th position derrière or 2nd position and may also be taken at 90 degrees.

Moderato

Battement fouetté en dehors from 4th position devant to 2nd position and en dedans from 4th position derrière to 2nd position in 2/4 time

ROND DE JAMBE JETE

A throwing action of the working leg which traces an arc through 2nd position.

This movement develops mobility and freedom in the hip socket.

From petite attitude devant, with the thigh at 45 degrees and the heel centred in front of the body, the leg is thrown to 2nd position at 90 degrees and continues to dégagé derrière à terre.

The technique required to execute the rond de jambe jeté is governed by the rotational action in the hip socket of the working leg.

The movement may be taken en dehors, commencing attitude devant and finishing in dégagé derrière, or en dedans commencing attitude derrière and finishing in dégagé devant.

Allegretto

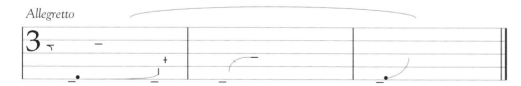

Rond de jambe jeté en dehors in 3/4 time

BATTEMENT FONDU WITH RISE

See *Foundations*, page 38.

A smoothly co-ordinated bending and stretching of both the working and the supporting leg incorporating a rise onto demi-pointe.

It is an essential exercise for developing strength and control for jumps.

From its position sur le cou-de-pied en fondu, the extension of the working leg through a small attitude to 45 or 90 degrees co-ordinates with the rise and stretch of the supporting leg.

When taken in a series, the working leg returns to its position sur le cou-de-pied en fondu while the supporting heel lowers slowly and smoothly.

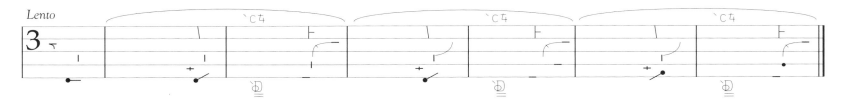

Battement fondu devant, to 2nd position, and derrière in 3/4 time

Note: Zoning information is used to indicate that the left knee (`C4) is slightly bent and that the heel of the left foot (`D) just skims the floor.

DOUBLE ROND DE JAMBE EN L'AIR

See *Foundations*, page 40.

A double circling action of the lower leg in which the foot begins and ends in 2nd position at 45 or 90 degrees.

When taken on a 3/4 rhythm, the double circling action is executed over the last two beats of a bar with the extension to 2nd position completed on the first beat of the next bar.

DOUBLE ROND DE JAMBE EN L'AIR EN DEHORS

Commencing with the working leg in 2nd position at 45 or 90 degrees, the lower leg performs two continuous outward circling actions with the turnout reinforced throughout: the toes trace a straight line inward to lightly touch the supporting leg, the heel leads a circular action slightly forward and outward until the lower leg is vertical, the toes retrace the straight line inward to lightly touch the supporting leg, and the heel leads the circular action outward again until the leg extends to 2nd position at 45 or 90 degrees.

Double rond de jambe en l'air en dehors at 45 degrees in 3/4 time

DOUBLE ROND DE JAMBE EN L'AIR EN DEDANS

Commencing with the working leg in 2nd position at 45 or 90 degrees, the lower leg performs two continuous inward circling actions with the turnout reinforced throughout: the heel of the working foot leads a circular action slightly forward and inward until the toes lightly touch the supporting leg, the toes trace a straight line until the lower leg is vertical, the heel again leads the circular action inward until the toes lightly touch the supporting leg, and the toes retrace the straight line outward until the leg extends to 2nd position at 45 or 90 degrees.

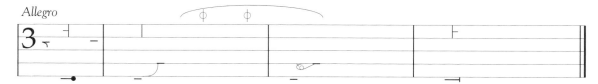

Double rond de jambe en l'air en dedans at 45 degrees in 3/4 time

PETIT BATTEMENT

See *Foundations*, page 41.

PETIT BATTEMENT WITH FULLY STRETCHED FOOT

A small sideways beating action of the working foot on the cou-de-pied of the supporting leg.

It is an exercise in accent, speed, and dexterity of the lower leg.

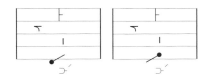

Petit battement starting position with fully stretched foot sur le cou-de-pied devant and derrière

PETITS BATTEMENTS SERRES - Continuous

A series of petits battements with the working foot either in petit battement position or fully stretched sur le cou-de-pied.

Allegro

Petits battements serrés in 2/4 time

PETITS BATTEMENTS BATTUS

A rapid sideways movement in which the fully stretched foot beats repeatedly in the same position either devant or derrière.

PETIT BATTEMENT BATTU DEVANT — toe to ankle · sideways

With the foot fully stretched sur le cou-de-pied devant, the lower leg opens sideways releasing sufficiently to execute a beating action sur le cou-de-pied devant.

PETIT BATTEMENT BATTU DERRIERE

With the foot fully stretched sur le cou-de-pied derrière, the lower leg opens sideways releasing sufficiently to execute a beating action sur le cou-de-pied derrière.

Allegro

Petits battements battus devant and derrière en demi-pointe in 2/4 time

CONTENTS
CHAPTER TWO: PORT DE BRAS

CHAPTER TWO
PORT DE BRAS

Ports de bras embody the expressive quality of simple beauty, as epitomised in the corps de ballet passages in *La Bayadère*, Act III, Kingdom of the Shades. They achieve their effect by combining the formal elements of classical line with the expressive elements of dynamic phrasing and musical interpretation. It is in ports de bras that key performance elements - initiation, flow, projection, and interpretation - are sensitively combined in the complete dancer.

The fundamental elements of ports de bras are introduced in *Foundations*, Chapter Three. Once the dancer understands and masters these, he or she may extend the use of the head and arms by including the body. By adding body bends and transfers of weight the dancer can sense the extremities of his or her reach and explore a fuller range of the air space around the body and limbs. This broadened spatial awareness expands the dancer's sphere of movement.

Awareness and control of posture is particularly important in advanced ports de bras since they incorporate a fuller range of torso actions and body shapes. In the port de bras section of class, the dancer first works on dynamic control of posture that provides the solid base from which broader head and arm movements are initiated. Good postural control frees the dancer to use breathing to enhance expression and quality of movement. As ports de bras are incorporated into more complex actions and enchaînements, this postural control allows greater use of the torso and broader changes of weight without disturbing the dancer's equilibrium. These in turn lead into travelling movements in the adage and allegro sections. Once again, however, it is important to avoid overly complex choreography and to retain the classical ideals of grace and elegance through formal simplicity, ease of execution, and quiet restraint.

Hand in hand with this conscious attention to physical control goes the cultivation of rhythmic sensibility. The elusive quality known as musicality involves much more than dancing on the beat. It is a personal, intuitive response that combines subtle co-ordination of the musical and the dance phrase. Since the interpretative element is inseparable from the musical phrasing and the motivation, it is important to select the right music to enhance the essential quality of a port de bras exercise.

Each musical time signature has its own shape and essence. For example, 2/4 meter is even, regular, symmetrical, and balanced, whereas 3/4 meter is rounded, lyrical, and lilting. This must be consciously understood and used to enhance the quality of the movement it underpins. Advanced ports de bras demonstrate the dancer's ability to shape a movement phrase and to complete it clearly, as well as his or her response to subtle degrees or gradations of dynamic accents and musical punctuation. Refer for more examples to *Examinations and Presentation Classes of the Royal Academy of Dance* (RAD 2001).

PORT DE BRAS

PORT DE BRAS WITH FORWARD BEND

En face, 1st position; arms 2nd position; head to 6:

The head turns slightly and the eyes follow the right hand as the lower abdominal muscles lift to initiate the forward bend. The arms lower toward 5th position as the bend increases through the upper lumbar spine. The pelvis tilts to complete the forward movement and the arms arrive in 5th position at the depth of the bend. The return to the upright position is a gradual unfolding action through the lumbar to thoracic spine, finishing with the head to 6. The gluteal muscles initiate the return, with the abdominal muscles strongly engaged until the movement is completed.

The inner thighs are used strongly throughout the movement to keep the weight centred over the feet and retain the turnout.

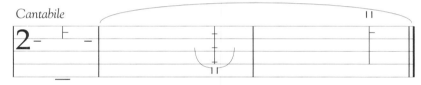

Port de bras with forward bend in 2/4 time

PORT DE BRAS WITH BACK BEND

En face, 1st position; arms 5th position; head to 6:

The back bend begins with a lengthening of the spine. The thoracic spine initiates the movement, taking with it the head and arms. As the back bend increases, so does the abdominal control. The bend may incorporate the use of the lumbar spine providing the position of the pelvis is stable. The head and eye line remain in front of the curve of the arm throughout the back bend.

The return to the upright position is initiated by stronger activation of the straight abdominal muscles. The torso lifts through the lumbar spine to the thoracic spine until the head completes the movement. At the same time, the arms move gradually from 5th position to arrive in 2nd position.

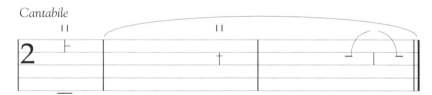

Port de bras with back bend in 2/4 time

PORT DE BRAS WITH SIDE BEND

En face, 1st position; arms 2nd position; head to 6:

The side bend begins with a lengthening of the spine, lifting the torso up and over. The oblique abdominal muscles retain the length in the back to control the side flexion, while the muscles below the shoulder blades stabilise the shoulder girdle. As the movement begins, the head is raised and turned slightly, with the eyes following the right hand as it lifts toward 5th position while the left arm lowers toward bras bas. As the movement continues, the head turns to complete the side bend with the eye line lowered over the left arm. The pelvis and shoulder girdle remain square throughout. As the body returns to the upright position, the arms move directly to 1st position before opening to 2nd position, with the eye line following the track of the right hand.

This movement may also be taken with the arms moving from 2nd to 4th position at the completion of the bend, with the head slightly turned and lowered to direct the eye line away from the raised arm. On the return to the upright position, the raised arm opens to 2nd position with the eye line following the track of the hand.

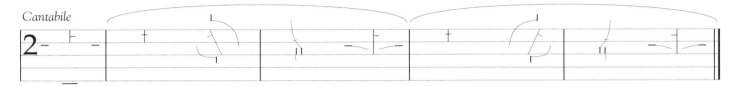

Port de bras with side bend in 2/4 time

REVERSE PORT DE BRAS WITH FORWARD BEND

En face, 1st position; arms 5th position; head to 6:

The head turns to 1 as the lower abdominal muscles lift to initiate the forward bending action. The movement proceeds through the upper lumbar spine and continues, allowing the pelvis to tilt and complete the forward bend.

The return to the upright position is a gradual unfolding action through the lumbar to thoracic spine. The gluteal muscles initiate the return with the abdominal muscles strongly engaged until the movement is completed. At the same time, the arms move through demi-seconde and arrive in 2nd position with the head to 6 on the completion of the movement.

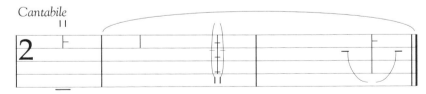

Reverse port de bras with forward bend in 2/4 time

REVERSE PORT DE BRAS WITH BACK BEND

En face, 1st position; arms 2nd position; head to 6:

The back bend begins with a lengthening of the spine while the shoulder girdle is held down. Keeping the trunk square, the thoracic spine then initiates the back bend and opening of the chest. The arms trace a line slightly behind the shoulders as the upper body bends backward. The bend incorporates the lumbar spine, with the position of the pelvis held stable. The head and eye line remain in front of the arms throughout the back bend.

The return to the upright position is initiated by strong use of the abdominal muscles, lifting through the lumbar spine to the thoracic spine. The hands trace an arc arriving in 5th position as the body arrives in the upright position.

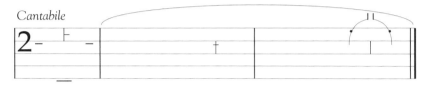

Reverse port de bras with back bend in 2/4 time

PORT DE BRAS WITH FORWARD AND BACK BEND IN 4TH POSITION EN FONDU

En face, 4th position en fondu right leg devant; arms 2nd position; head to 6:

The forward movement is initiated by lifting the lower abdominal muscles and, as the body bends, the arms lower toward 5th position with the eyes following the right hand. The arms remain in 5th position on the return to the upright position, with the majority of the weight retained on the front leg.

Keeping the arms in 5th position, the head turns to 6 as the backward movement is initiated by lengthening the spine and lifting the torso up and over. Retaining stability in the pelvis with the weight over the front leg, the whole spine makes a controlled and lengthened back bend. The torso returns to the upright position by use of the abdominal muscles, and the arms open to 2nd position with the head returning to 1.

When taken on a 3/4 or 4/4 rhythm, the arms and body move continuously through 4 bars: one bar for the forward bend, one bar to return to the upright position, one bar for the back bend, and one bar to return to the upright position.

This may also be taken with a reverse port de bras action.

Port de bras with forward and back bend in 4th position en fondu in 3/4 time

CIRCULAR PORT DE BRAS

En croisé, 5th position right foot devant; arms 4th position left arm raised; head to 1:

The head turns to 5 as the lower abdominal muscles lift to initiate the forward bend. The eye focus lowers as the forward bend continues to its depth. The body is then drawn upwards into a side bend to the left, with the pelvis and shoulders retained square. During the side flexion, the head turns to direct the eye focus over the left hand as it moves to 2nd position while the right arm makes a full port de bras to 5th position. From the side bend, the thoracic and lumbar spine extend to continue into a back bend with the head lifting slightly to complement the inclination in the upper spine. As the body continues into the opposite side bend, the arms sweep sideways to 4th position with the left arm raised. The trunk then returns to the upright position and the eyes re-focus to 1.

When taken on a 3/4 rhythm, the arms and body move continuously through four bars: one bar for the forward bend, one bar for the side bend, one bar for the back bend, and one bar to complete the movement.

When taken at the barre, the eyes follow the line of the hand as the arm lowers to 5th position with the forward bend.

Cantabile

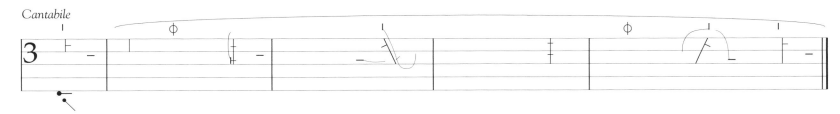

Circular port de bras in 3/4 time

CIRCULAR PORT DE BRAS WITH TRANSFER OF WEIGHT

En croisé, left foot dégagé derrière; arms 4th position left arm raised; head to 1:

The use of the body and arms is the same as in circular port de bras. The weight is transferred through demi-plié with the forward bend and into dégagé devant with the side bend. The circular movement of the body and arms continues, with the position of the legs retained to finish in croisé devant.

Cantabile

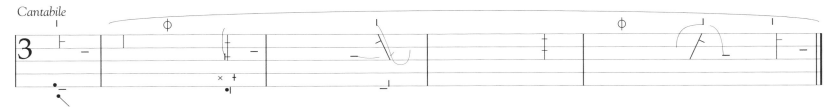

Circular port de bras with transfer of weight in 3/4 time

CIRCULAR PORT DE BRAS IN 4TH POSITION EN FONDU

En face, 4th position en fondu right leg devant; arms 4th position left arm raised; head to 6:

The use of the body and arms is the same as in circular port de bras and the weight placement and control of the pelvis reflect the technique of port de bras with forward and back bend in 4th position en fondu. Stability is retained in the pelvis, with the weight over the front leg throughout.

Cantabile

Circular port de bras in 4th position en fondu in 3/4 time

CONTENTS
CHAPTER THREE: CENTRE PRACTICE

CHAPTER THREE
CENTRE PRACTICE

As explained in *Foundations*, Chapter Four, exercises performed in the centre practice section of a class are not just a repetition of barre work. From the beginning of dance training, selected barre movements may be replicated without the aid of the barre to build balance, strength and stamina. Beyond sheer repetition, centre practice adds the important element of presentation. Advanced centre practice combines barre exercises in a variety of ways to produce sequences that blend a number of elements, always focusing outward to connect the dancer with the performance area and audience. Balance, control, co-ordination, alignment and spatial awareness all come into play. Movements are connected by linking steps to create seamless dance phrases that form the basis for adage and allegro enchaînements and, ultimately, choreographed variations.

The definitions included in this chapter continue from the Basic Definitions introduced in *Foundations*, page 16. They present Dynamic and Spatial Values which add variety and interest to more advanced movements. A basic arabesque, for example, may be elongated into an allongé line. An adage sequence may extend and suspend a simple weight transfer to produce a tombé quality, and a series of jetés may be taken élancé or en manège to cover more of the performance space.

CENTRE PRACTICE

DYNAMIC AND SPATIAL VALUES

Positions and steps can be embellished with various movement qualities or dynamics, which add richness, breadth and colour.

ALLONGE

Term used to describe an extended line in which the body is pitched forward and the spine lengthened.

PIQUE

Term used to describe a quick action performed with a sharp, light quality.

ELANCE

Term used to describe steps which are performed with a swift, darting quality.

TOMBE

Term used to describe a transfer of weight taken with a quality of suspension, from a straight supporting leg with the extended leg en l'air leading into a position en fondu.

TERRE A TERRE

Phrase used to describe a movement executed close to the ground, mainly through the action of the ankles and feet.

EN MANEGE

Phrase used to describe a series of movements executed along a circular path around the stage.

CONTENTS
CHAPTER FOUR: PIROUETTES

CHAPTER FOUR
PIROUETTES

Perhaps the most famous pirouettes in the classical repertoire are Odile's 32 fouettés in *Swan Lake*, Act III. Here, the seductive Black Swan's continuous spinning mesmerises both Siegfried and the audience. Although pirouettes must appear effortless and spontaneous, mastering their technique requires a long and gradual build-up, beginning with the skills introduced in *Foundations*, Chapter Five, Turning Movements.

The dancer begins by learning pirouettes sur place, then turns that travel en diagonale and, in their advanced form, pirouettes en manège (i.e. travelling around the stage along a circular path). This sequence prepares the dancer for professional choreography: it mirrors the structure of many classical variations that begin with stationary turns and culminate in a series of spins that traverse the stage before spiralling inward to achieve a bravura climax. This structure completes the typical Petipa male variation such as that of Prince Florimund in *Sleeping Beauty*, Act III, or female variation, such as Aurora's in *Sleeping Beauty*, Act III, Wedding Scene.

At more advanced stages of training, the dancer works to achieve multiple pirouettes. This requires attention to initiating the turn, prolonging the spin, and completing it cleanly and securely.

Good initiation involves co-ordinated sequence and timing of legs, arms, head, and torso. The additional force required for a multiple turn comes from a strong push-off from the legs, synchronised with the impetus of the head and arm, and co-ordinated with a strong centring of the torso. The form of a pirouette and the use of the arms do not differ for single versus multiple turns. For example, no lead arm is used for turns en dehors, except in fouetté rond de jambe en tournant.

To sustain the spin, the dancer quickly achieves a stable turning position. Whereas a compact position facilitates a speedy turn, an extended position yields a slower turn, given equal force of push-off. The dancer therefore learns to adjust the force of push-off to accommodate a range of different turning positions. A secure position prolongs the turn. The dancer learns to maintain the turning position by suspending it throughout the prolonged spin. Eye focus (spotting) is particularly important for control of dynamic equilibrium in multiple turns. Since the head concentrates a relatively great mass, it can throw off the dancer's balance if it is not held vertical, close to the axis of rotation throughout the spin. The turn must appear to stop as effortlessly and cleanly as it began. To achieve a clean and exact completion, the dancer suspends the position just before the end of the turn. Since an advanced pirouette may finish in a variety of positions, achieving this suspension is particularly important. It builds the control that allows the dancer to move seamlessly into the next transition and prepares the dancer for complex choreography in which a spin may lead into an open position or off-balance action. The final ending in a series of turns makes a particularly strong statement, since the audience always remembers the last position.

Using musical dynamics can assist the performance of pirouettes. It is important to time the preparation and to use the phrasing to assist in the impetus for the turn. The dancer learns to anticipate the pulse to hit the high point of the movement with the musical accent. The musical impulse is also used to link the three phases of a pirouette. The broader the shape in which the turn is taken, the faster the limbs must move in order to reach the selected position as the turn is initiated. The timing of the legs and arms must be well synchronised. In pirouettes performed with a change of position during the turn, the body configuration can be sustained or changed rhythmically to control the rate of turn (narrowing increases speed, widening decreases it) throughout the transitions from initiation to spin to completion.

This chapter contains word descriptions and Benesh Movement Notation examples showing a single turn, but at more advanced levels these may be taken with multiple turns. Pirouettes finishing in open positions of the legs may incorporate various positions of the arms, poses and alignments (introduced in *Foundations*, pages 17-20). All pirouettes for the female dancer may be taken en pointe. Pirouettes for the male dancer are taken with a strong rise as opposed to a relevé. The speed and quality of the turn will vary according to the time signature and type of enchaînement (i.e. adage or allegro).

FLIC-FLAC

An action consisting of two sharply accented inward brushing movements of the working leg.

En face, right leg extended to 2nd position at glissé height; arms 2nd position:

As the lower leg moves inward and the arms lower to bras bas, the ball of the foot brushes the floor and the foot passes through a fully stretched position sur le cou-de-pied derrière. The lower leg then opens slightly to allow a second brushing action to cou-de-pied devant while the supporting foot begins to rise and the arms lift through 1st position. The rise is completed as the leg extends to 2nd position at glissé height and the arms reach 2nd position.

Flic-flac derrière-devant may also be taken in reverse, devant-derrière.

Initially this movement may be prepared at the barre without the rising action.

The combination of the two inward actions and the extension of the working leg are taken in one count.

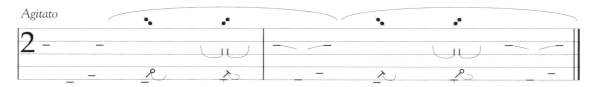

Flic-flac derrière-devant and devant-derrière in 6/8 time

FLIC-FLAC EN TOURNANT EN DEHORS

En face, right leg extended to 2nd position at glissé height; arms 2nd position:

With a swivelling action making a 1/4-turn en dehors, the lower leg moves inward with the ball of the foot brushing the floor and the foot then passes through a fully stretched position sur le cou-de-pied derrière. The arms lower to bras bas with the inward action. Continuing to turn en dehors, the lower leg opens slightly to allow an inward brushing action to cou-de-pied devant, as the supporting heel releases and the arms lift to 1st position. The rise and full turn are completed simultaneously, as the working leg extends to 2nd position at glissé height and the arms open to 2nd position.

The movement may be executed in reverse with the turning action taken en dedans.

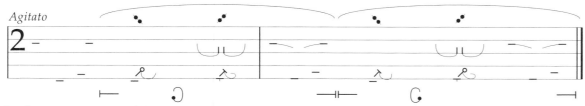

Flic-flac en tournant en dehors and en dedans in 6/8 time

PIROUETTES

PIROUETTE EN DEHORS WITH ARMS IN 5TH POSITION
See *Foundations*, page 73.

From the initial preparatory position, the arms are raised directly to 5th position with the relevé action. The arms remain in 5th position on closing en demi-plié after the completion of the turn.

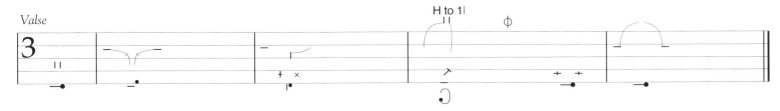

Pirouette en dehors with arms in 5th position in 3/4 time

PIROUETTE EN DEDANS WITHOUT FOUETTE WITH ARMS IN 5TH POSITION
See *Foundations*, page 74.

From the initial preparatory position, the arms are raised directly to 5th position with the relevé action. The arms remain in 5th position on closing en demi-plié after the completion of the turn.

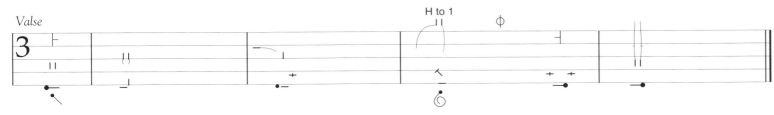

Pirouette en dedans without fouetté with arms in 5th position in 3/4 time

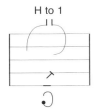

Note: The zoning information "H to 1" indicates that the head spots to the front.
Spotting may apply beyond the current frame when indicated, for example, by the use of an asterisk (*) or an end bracket (⊢), e.g. see pages 45 and 46.

PIROUETTE EN DEDANS WITH FOUETTE WITH ARMS IN 5TH POSITION
See *Foundations*, page 74.

From the initial preparatory position, the leading arm opens toward 2nd position and is immediately joined by the other to form 5th position with the relevé action. The arms remain in 5th position on closing en demi-plié after the completion of the turn.

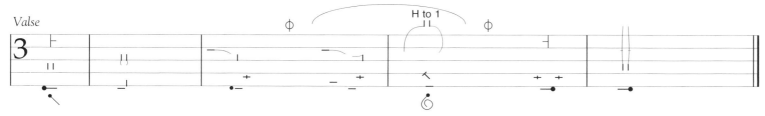

Pirouette en dedans with fouetté with arms in 5th position in 3/4 time

PIROUETTE EN DEHORS FINISHING IN 4TH POSITION EN FONDU
See *Foundations*, page 73.

After the turn is completed, the raised leg moves directly to 4th position derrière while the supporting heel lowers, simultaneously and with control, to end en fondu. The arms reach the selected finishing position as the movement is completed.

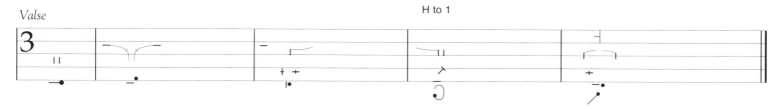

Pirouette en dehors finishing in 4th position en fondu in 3/4 time

PIROUETTE EN DEHORS AND EN DEDANS FINISHING IN AN OPEN POSITION EN L'AIR

After the turn is completed, the raised leg moves directly to its designated position while the supporting heel lowers, simultaneously and with control. The arms reach the selected finishing position as the movement is completed.

When the pirouette finishes in attitude derrière or arabesque, the working leg makes a passé action in order to reach its final position. (See Adage section, développé passé, page 54.)

Pirouettes ending in open positions may also be taken finishing en fondu.

Cantabile

Pirouette en dehors finishing in attitude derrière in 6/8 time

PIROUETTE EN DEHORS IN AN OPEN POSITION

Pirouettes may be taken in various positions.

From a demi-plié in 4th position with the majority of the weight over the front foot, the movement is initiated by taking the leg and arms directly and immediately to their position en l'air, combined with a strong relevé on the supporting leg. The squareness of the trunk and shoulders must be secured as soon as possible in order to establish the selected position by the first quarter of the turn. The pirouette finishes on a straight supporting leg or en fondu with the selected position retained.

When the pirouette is taken in 2nd position en l'air, the preparation is usually from 2nd position.

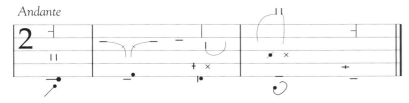

Andante

Pirouette en dehors in attitude derrière in 2/4 time

PIROUETTE EN DEDANS IN AN OPEN POSITION

Pirouettes may be taken in various positions.

From 4th position en fondu, the movement is initiated by taking the leg and arms directly and immediately to their position en l'air, combined with a strong relevé on the supporting leg. The squareness of the trunk and shoulders must be secured as soon as possible in order to establish the selected position by the first quarter of the turn. The pirouette finishes on a straight supporting leg or en fondu with the selected position retained.

Barcarolle
Poco allegro

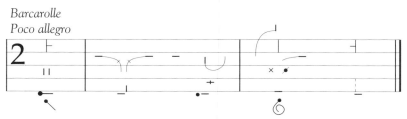

Pirouette en dedans in attitude derrière in 6/8 time

PETIT SOUTENU

Commencing in corner 8, en croisé, right foot dégagé devant; arms 3rd position right arm forward; head to 6, eye focus remains to 6 throughout:

With a fondu on the supporting leg, the extended leg is released just off the ground to make a small rond de jambe en dehors into a posé en demi-pointe, and the incoming leg closes immediately into 5th position devant making a 1/2-turn. The turning action continues with a change of feet to finish facing 5.

From 3rd position, the right arm opens with the rond de jambe action. As the left leg closes into 5th position devant, the left arm immediately joins the right to form pirouette position.

The impetus for the turn comes from a push-off from the fondu with a quick transfer of weight into the posé en demi-pointe, and the co-ordinated use of the arms.

H to 6 to end
Allegro

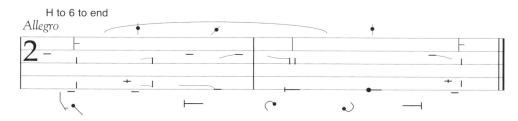

Petit soutenu in 2/4 time

PETIT PAS DE BASQUE EN TOURNANT

Commencing in corner 8, en croisé, right foot dégagé devant; arms 3rd position right arm forward; head to 6, eye focus remains to 6 throughout:

With a fondu on the supporting leg, the extended leg is released just off the ground to make a small rond de jambe en dehors springing lightly into a posé en demi-pointe. The incoming leg lifts slightly to make a small rond de jambe en dedans closing into 5th position devant en demi-pointes, completing a 1/2-turn. The turning action continues with a change of feet to finish facing 5.

From 3rd position, the right arm opens with the first rond de jambe action. As the left leg closes into 5th position devant, the left arm immediately joins the right to form pirouette position.

The impetus for the turn comes from a push-off from the fondu with a quick transfer of weight into the posé, and the co-ordinated use of the arms.

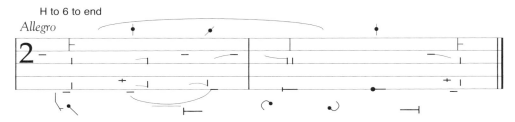

Petit pas de basque en tournant in 2/4 time

FOUETTE ROND DE JAMBE EN TOURNANT

A pirouette incorporating a whipping action of the working leg.

En face, right leg 4th position devant en l'air en fondu; arms 3rd position right arm forward:

From 4th position devant, the movement is initiated by a whipping action of the extended leg which moves through 2nd to pirouette position, combined with a strong relevé on the supporting leg leading into a pirouette en dehors.

From 3rd position, the right arm opens toward 2nd position with the working leg and is immediately joined by the left arm to form pirouette position. To finish the movement, the left arm opens to 2nd position as the right leg extends to 4th position devant en l'air en fondu.

Stability and balance are maintained through strong control of the pelvis and spine.

The impetus for the turn is a combination of the leg and arm action. The muscles below the shoulder blades hold the shoulders in place to support the thoracic spine and allow ease of action of the head.

When taken in a series, the fouetté rond de jambe may be prepared with a pas de bourrée en tournant en dedans or a pirouette en dehors.

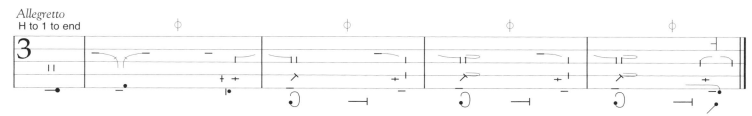

Fouetté rond de jambe en tournant prepared with pirouette en dehors in 3/4 time

POSE PIROUETTE EN DEHORS

Commencing in corner 8, en croisé, right foot dégagé devant; arms 3rd position right arm forward; head to 6, eye focus remaining to 6 throughout:

With a step to 4th position en fondu toward corner 6, the back leg is released just off the ground to make a small rond de jambe en dedans leading into a posé en avant en demi-pointe. The right leg is immediately drawn up to pirouette position as the turn continues en dehors to finish facing 5.

From 3rd position, the leading arm moves toward 2nd position with the step to 4th position en fondu, and is immediately joined by the other arm to form pirouette position with the posé.

When taken in a series, the pirouette finishes with a tombé en avant facing the direction of travel in order to continue the next turn.

Quick march

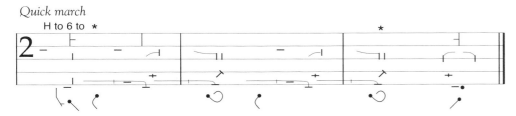

Posé pirouette en dehors in 2/4 time

CHAINE

Commencing in corner 8, en croisé, right foot dégagé devant; arms 3rd position right arm forward; head to 6, eye focus remaining to 6 throughout:

From a fondu and with a step onto demi-pointe in a small 2nd position, the weight is transferred onto the right leg with a 1/2-turn en dedans. The weight is then transferred onto the left leg in 1st position, completing the turn en dehors.

From 3rd position, the leading arm opens toward 2nd position with the initial step and is immediately joined by the other arm to form 1st position.

When taken in a series, each step makes a 1/2-turn and the arms and legs remain in 1st position.

Galop

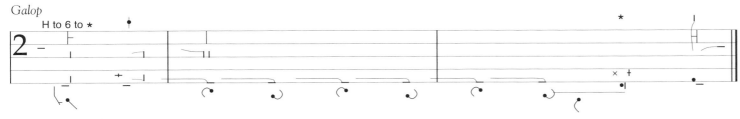

Chaîné turns in 2/4 time

PIROUETTE IN 2ND POSITION EN DEHORS WITH PETITS SAUTES

A turning action in an open position combined with petits sautés.

En face, right leg 2nd position en l'air at 90 degrees; arms 2nd position:

While the turning action occurs, the supporting leg makes a series of small hops retaining flexion in the ankle with the sole of the foot close to the floor. The arms are held in 2nd position throughout.

Stability is maintained through strong control of the pelvis and trunk keeping both sides of the body equally held, with particular attention to the supporting side. Care is needed to maintain and sustain the height and placing of the raised leg. The muscles below the shoulder blades hold the shoulder girdle in place maintaining the position of the arms in 2nd position and allowing ease of action of the head.

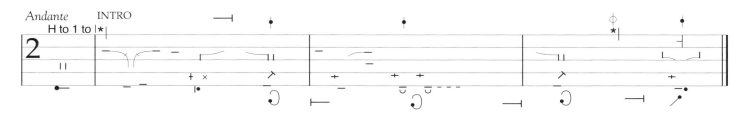

Pirouette in 2nd position en dehors with petits sautés prepared and ended with a single pirouette en dehors in 2/4 time

CONTENTS
CHAPTER FIVE: ADAGE

CHAPTER FIVE
ADAGE

The basic principles of adage are outlined in *Foundations*, Chapter Six. The more advanced movements selected for inclusion in this chapter can also be incorporated into the allegro and pointe work sections of class. When mastered on demi-pointe, certain movements described here can also be done on pointe in preparation for pas de deux work, e.g. fouetté of adage. Movements practised in the adage section of class to develop precision of the limbs in space may ultimately be used in allegro. They must first be co-ordinated in adage to prepare for their use in allegro.

Leg extensions are described at the full classical height of 90 degrees but can be taken higher, though only when appropriate and without distorting the purity of line. In adage work, it is important for the dancer to focus on the process by which the limbs reach their full extension rather than on how high the leg goes. This involves the quality of sustaining and lengthening the limbs outward, radiating from the centre of the whole body. Classical leg extensions achieve their beauty shaped by the dancer's breathing, as an expression of spiritual expansiveness, never by force or strain.

The adage section of a more advanced class prepares the dancer for more complex co-ordination, using all alignments and directions of travel, a fuller range of body poses, and different ways in which the limbs can move in space from one position to another. This greater complexity requires greater co-ordination, balance, control, and concentration. It also requires greater strength to perform more intricate movements with the appearance of ease. Advanced adage work is characterised by balanced harmony of limbs and torso, always retaining simplicity of line – qualities epitomised in such classic gems as the Adage (*Giselle*, Act II) or the Rose Adagio (*Sleeping Beauty*, Act I). Simplicity of line is crucial to the performance of choreography as technically demanding as, for example, Princess Aurora's series of supported attitude promenades and balances. Aesthetically, if the limbs are not balanced, the line is distorted and the essence of the movement destroyed. The dancer achieves this difficult feat through concentration and a clear understanding of the classical line, rather than through sheer strength.

FOUETTE OF ADAGE EN L'AIR

See *Foundations*, page 67.

A fully co-ordinated movement in which the body turns away from the raised leg with a pivoting action of the supporting leg.

This can be executed with various arm positions and alignments.

FOUETTE OF ADAGE EN L'AIR WITH 1/2-TURN

Facing 2, right leg 4th position devant en l'air at 90 degrees; arms 5th position:

With a pivoting action of the supporting leg, the body makes a 1/2-turn away from the raised leg. Rotating in its hip socket, the leg passes through 2nd position en face retaining its height with the arms remaining in 5th position. The pivoting action continues with the leg gradually adjusting its position behind the hip, while the arms open to finish in 1st arabesque facing 4.

The muscles of the upper back are strongly held throughout. From the en face position, heightened awareness of a lift in the upper body enables the arms to move gradually from the curved to the extended line.

This movement may be executed with a relevé action.

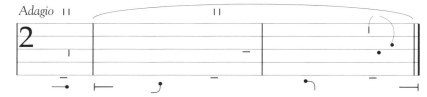

Fouetté of adage en l'air with 1/2-turn in 2/4 time

GRAND FOUETTE RELEVE EN TOURNANT

A composite step consisting of a grand battement relevé in 2nd position and a fouetté relevé with a 1/2-turn.

En croisé, right foot dégagé derrière; bras bas; head to 1:

From dégagé derrière, the right leg brushes through 1st position en demi-plié into a strong relevé on the left leg with the right leg making a battement to 2nd position at 90 degrees facing 5. The arms co-ordinate with and assist the action by moving through 1st position on the demi-plié and into 2nd position on the battement relevé, with the head to 6.

With a swivelling action to face 8, the raised leg brushes through 1st position en demi-plié and the arms move through bras bas to 1st position with the eye focus to 8. There is a strong relevé on the left leg, with the right leg making a battement to 4th position devant and the arms raised to 5th position. The strong fouetté action and 1/2-turn of the body occur with a lift in the upper body and through use of both sides of the trunk, especially the muscles on the side of the raised leg. Engaging the gluteal muscles on the supporting side ensures and reinforces the turnout of the supporting leg as the pelvis rotates. The movement is completed in 2nd arabesque en fondu.

When taken on a 3/4 rhythm, the battement to 2nd position occurs on the anacrusis, the swivel and brush through 1st position occur on the first beat of the first bar, and the movement is completed on the first beat of the second bar.

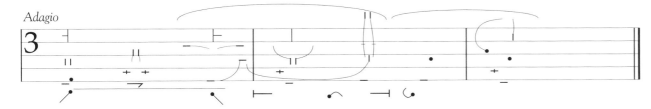

Grand fouetté relevé en tournant in 3/4 time

ROTATION EN L'AIR

See *Foundations*, page 68.

A fully co-ordinated movement in which the body turns toward the raised leg with a pivoting action of the supporting leg.

This can be executed with various arm positions and alignments.

ROTATION EN L'AIR AT 90 DEGREES WITH 1/2-TURN

Facing 4, 1st arabesque at 90 degrees, standing on the left leg:

The movement is made with a pivoting action of the supporting leg en dehors while the body makes a 1/4-turn toward the raised leg. Rotating in its hip socket, the leg gradually adjusts to 2nd position en face retaining its height, while the arms move to 5th position. The pivoting action continues making a further 1/4-turn, and the raised leg finishes in 4th position devant facing 2.

The first 1/4-turn of the action requires strong use of the abdominal muscles to bring the torso into its upright position.

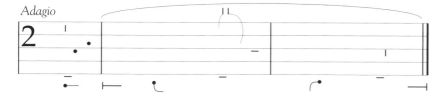

Rotation en l'air at 90 degrees with 1/2-turn in 2/4 time

ARABESQUE PENCHEE

An arabesque incorporating a sustained tilt of the body.

Facing 2, 1st arabesque at 90 degrees, standing on the right leg:

The movement is initiated from the supporting hip, and control of the body weight during the tilting action comes from strong use of the hamstring and gluteal muscles on the supporting side. Weight is retained over the forefoot and, in order for the tilt to occur, there is a slightly reduced degree of turnout on the supporting leg. The pelvis must remain as square as possible and, as the leg lifts and the tilt increases, any rotation toward the working leg must be carefully controlled by strong use of the abdominal muscles.

Return to the upright position is controlled by the back extensor muscles.

The arabesque line and the curve of the back are retained throughout the tilting action and recovery to the upright position, with both sides of the torso remaining equally lengthened and supported.

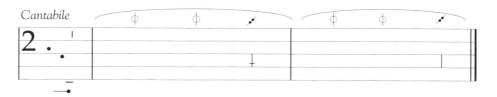

Arabesque penchée in 6/8 time

BATTEMENT LENT

A sustained lifting and lowering of the working leg.

From 5th position, the leg passes through battement tendu and, lengthening away from the body, is raised slowly to its maximum height. The leg is then lowered slowly, passing through battement tendu to close in 5th position.

When taken on a 3/4 rhythm, the leg moves continuously through four bars.

BATTEMENT LENT DEVANT

The movement requires correct weight placement through a stable and controlled supporting leg and a lengthening of the whole spine. As the leg lifts, the abdominal muscles are further activated to stabilise the pelvis and lumbar spine, facilitating strong use of the hip flexor muscles.

BATTEMENT LENT TO 2ND POSITION

Special attention is required to sustain the squareness of the pelvis, turnout of the working leg, and lift out of the supporting hip.

BATTEMENT LENT DERRIERE

The gluteal muscles, hamstrings, and inner thigh muscles are strongly engaged. The raising of the leg necessitates the tilting of the pelvis, thus curving the lumbar spine and allowing the forward counterbalance of the upper body. This is controlled by the abdominal muscles and strong use of the upper back. The perpendicular line of the supporting leg should be retained throughout with both sides of the body fully lengthened. As the leg makes its controlled descent to 5th position, the spine is lengthened and the pelvis is adjusted to resume the upright position.

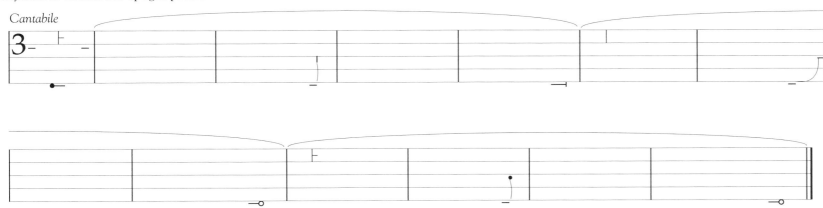

Battement lent devant, to 2nd position, and derrière in 3/4 time

ENVELOPPE

A controlled incoming movement of the raised working leg in which the toes trace a straight line from 4th position devant into retiré devant, from 2nd position into retiré, or from 4th position derrière into retiré derrière, before closing in 5th position.

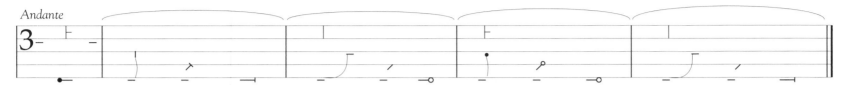

Grand battement closing with enveloppé en croix in 3/4 time

DEVELOPPE PASSE

See *Foundations*, page 44.

An enveloppé and développé action passing through retiré position.

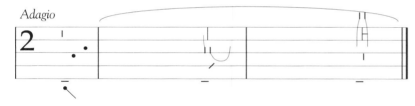

Développé passé from 1st arabesque in 2/4 time

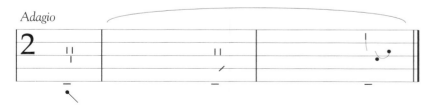

Développé passé to 1st arabesque in 2/4 time

BALLOTTE

A rocking movement in which the weight is transferred from one foot to the other, incorporating an enveloppé and développé action.

BALLOTTE DESSOUS AND DESSUS

Facing 6, left leg 4th position derrière en l'air at 90 degrees en fondu; arms 3rd position right arm forward; eye focus over the right forearm:

Ballotté dessous: from 4th position derrière, while the left leg makes an enveloppé action to retiré derrière and the trunk adjusts to the upright position, the right leg straightens simultaneously to end en demi-pointe. At the same time, the right arm opens toward 2nd position as the left arm moves toward 1st position and the head turns toward 1. The left leg then closes to 5th position derrière en demi-pointes and the right leg is immediately drawn up through retiré devant to execute a développé devant finishing en fondu. The upper body inclines slightly backward as the arms arrive in 3rd position with the left arm forward and the head to 1 at the completion of the movement.

Ballotté dessus: from 4th position devant, while the right leg makes an enveloppé action to retiré devant and the trunk adjusts to the upright position, the left leg straightens simultaneously to end en demi-pointe. At the same time, the left arm opens toward 2nd position as the right arm moves toward 1st position and the head turns toward the right arm. The right leg then closes to 5th position devant en demi-pointes and the left leg is immediately drawn up through retiré derrière to execute a développé derrière finishing en fondu. The upper body inclines slightly forward as the arms arrive in 3rd position with the right arm forward and the eye focus over the right forearm at the completion of the movement.

The adjustment of the body weight necessary to achieve the rocking action requires balance over the supporting leg and control from a strong centre.

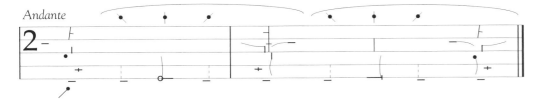

Ballotté dessous and dessus in 2/4 time

RENVERSE

A turning action used in adagio and allegro movements in which the dancer appears to lose balance momentarily.

En croisé, 5th position en demi-pointes, right foot devant; bras bas; head to 1:

The first 1/4-turn commences to the left with a slight side bend to the right, and the upper back extends into a back bend with the eye focus retained to 1. The body continues to turn as the spine arches into a full back bend, sustaining the eye focus to 1 as much as possible. The 1/2-turn to 6 completes the détourné action rapidly, in order to restore balance and return the body to its upright position.

The spiralling action of the torso involves as much range of movement as muscular control allows. The back bend is controlled by strong use of the lower abdominal muscles and the shoulder girdle is pulled well down during the turn.

The legs change from 5th position to 5th position finishing with the left foot devant, co-ordinating with the turning action.

The dancer appears to be momentarily off-balance just after the first 1/4-turn.

Adagio

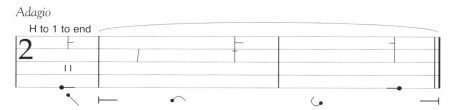

Renversé in 2/4 time

GRAND ROND DE JAMBE EN L'AIR AND PAS DE BOURREE DESSOUS EN TOURNANT WITH A RENVERSE ACTION

See *Foundations*, page 48.

En croisé, right leg sur le cou-de-pied derrière en fondu; arms 3rd position left arm forward:

The movement commences with a coupé dessous, arms through 1st position, into grand rond de jambe relevé to 4th position derrière at 90 degrees, and lowers en fondu facing 5. With maximum lift in the spine, the arms move through 5th position as the leg passes through 2nd position en face. The arms arrive in 2nd position as the leg arrives in 4th position derrière, while the chest opens and the head inclines and turns to 1.

The renversé action commences with the first step of the pas de bourrée en tournant. On the 1/4-turn to face 8 the legs pull up to 5th position en demi-pointes and the arms move toward bras bas as the sideways bend and spiralling action commence. Continuing with a 1/2-turn to face 6, the recovery from the back bend into the upright position occurs as the right foot steps into a small 2nd position and the arms move through bras bas to 1st position. To complete the pas de bourrée, the left leg closes into 5th position devant en demi-plié as the arms open to 2nd position with the head to 1.

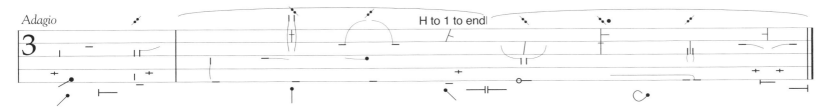

Grand rond de jambe en l'air and pas de bourrée dessous en tournant with a renversé action in 9/8 time

CONTENTS

CHAPTER SIX: ALLEGRO

CONTENTS

CHAPTER SIX: ALLEGRO

CONTENTS
CHAPTER SIX: ALLEGRO

The bounding springs and soaring leaps of allegro work embody the essence of spiritual and physical flight. This is poetically expressed in *Sleeping Beauty*, Act III, when the Bluebird dazzles Princess Florine with his rebounding vaults, enticing her to escape her confinement and ascend to his realm far above the earth.

The basic principles of allegro are introduced in *Foundations*, Chapter Seven. These comprise a well-timed and directed push-off, a clearly presented aerial position, and a controlled, sustained landing. Nowadays, with choreographers making increasing demands and expecting the dancer to take ever greater risks, it is all the more necessary that he or she masters the basic technique. Secure basics will help him or her make that progression and take the choreography to further extremes. The initiation of each jump must be precise and concise, using as much effort as is needed and no more, with the sequence and timing of the arms well co-ordinated with the legs. In the air, the female dancer must be able to achieve all kinds of aerial shapes, even turning en l'air, while the male dancer must be able to sustain and suspend his position with no apparent effort, creating a vivid image at the height of the jump. The landing of bigger travelled jumps must be cushioned through the co-ordinated sequence and timing of limbs and torso, making a brilliant visual picture. As in a series of pirouettes, the final landing in a series of jumps makes a particularly strong statement, and must be especially solid and secure.

Building from good basics, advanced allegro comprises jumps that are more complex in themselves and that may be embellished and arranged in a variety of combinations. Arm positions may be varied, as may the movement dynamics. For example, the simple form of an assemblé is refined so that the legs assemble in the air before landing. It may be taken élancé, with broad travel in any direction, and complemented by different alignments of the body, arms, and head. Beats may be added, as may changes of direction and turns en l'air. The assemblé itself may embody a range of qualities from the quicksilver lightness of a petit assemblé through the soaring vaults of a grand assemblé élancé. At the advanced level, petit allegro through grand allegro steps may be linked in phrases that display a wide array of dynamic qualities, with each movement retaining its distinct flavour. To extend the span of allegro enchaînements, jumps may be linked in sequences that cross the stage from corner to corner en diagonale, or that curve around the entire stage en manège.

Advanced batterie builds on the principles of beaten jumps introduced in *Foundations*, page 98, in that the legs open slightly before a beat. When an allegro step is embellished with a beat, the fundamental step must be a replica of the original. For example, when a jeté ordinaire incorporates a beat, there is no change in the height of the leg on the preparatory brush, and the landing position is the same as if there were no beat.

Although there are no new categories of allegro, at this level petit, medium, and grand allegro are interwoven to produce more richly textured dance phrases. Terre à terre jumps, those performed close to the ground through resilience mainly in the feet and ankles, may alternate with steps of high elevation involving the entire body. Lyrical ports de bras may be juxtaposed with bounding vaults to add highlight and surprise. This is clearly illustrated in the first phrase of the first Male Variation of the Peasant Pas de Deux, *Giselle*, Act I, in which a pas de bourrée and chassé lead into a cabriole derrière in 1st arabesque. Here the continuous head, arm, and torso movement contrasts with the strongly punctuated pas de bourrée and leads into a bounding, energised cabriole. The dancer learns to use controlled gradations of energy so that the dynamics of each action remain as they should be. The fluctuations within each chain of movements punctuate the dynamic phrasing. Because of the many different ways in which steps can be linked, it is even more important to study the values of each step individually before putting them together.

To achieve the different qualities of steps from petit to grand allegro, the dancer must understand the degree of energy needed for each, and use only as much as required. For example, the more impetus on push-off the more control will be needed on landing. Large jumps require more energy and vitality from initiation to completion. The use of the head and eye focus, so vital in turns, is also important in allegro work to give clarity to the line of a jump, to enliven or enhance it. This involves the use of projection and animated use of the eyes in order to engage with the audience. Finally, the dancer's interpretation comes from total body involvement and the use of breath and projection to convey the motivation for each movement.

ASSEMBLE DE COTE

See *Foundations*, page 83.

A travelling jump in which the legs are assembled, fully stretched, in 5th position in the air before landing, and the body weight is transferred with the action of the legs.

ASSEMBLE DE COTE DESSUS

En face, 5th position right foot derrière; bras bas:

As the demi-plié commences, the back foot begins to slide toward 2nd position. The combination of the sliding action and strong push-off from the supporting leg provides the force to spring into the air, travel sideways and assemble the legs, fully stretched in 5th position with the right foot devant at the height of the jump, before landing en demi-plié.

The arms make a basic port de bras to reach 2nd position at the height of the jump, and retain the position on landing.

This movement may also be performed dessous, en avant, and en arrière with varying arm positions, and requires a travelling preparatory step such as a glissade.

Non troppo allegro

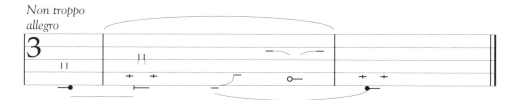

Assemblé de côté dessus prepared by glissade derrière in 3/4 time

ASSEMBLE DESSUS EN TOURNANT

See *Foundations*, page 83.

An assemblé dessus which turns in the air.

Facing 7, right foot dégagé devant; arms 2nd position:

The movement commences with a running pas de bourrée into 4th position en demi-plié, right foot devant. The left foot then brushes through 1st position and, with a 1/4-turn, continues into a battement toward 2nd position, pushing vertically into the air. The legs immediately join in 5th position with the left foot devant and the turn continues. The movement finishes en demi-plié facing 6.

From 2nd position, the arms make a full port de bras arriving in 5th position at the height of the jump and remain in 5th position on the landing. The swift turning action requires the eyes to focus to 6 as soon as possible after the push into the air.

The movement may be taken with more than one turn in the air.

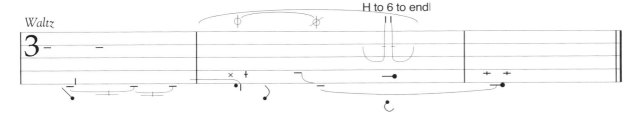

Assemblé dessus en tournant prepared by a running pas de bourrée in 3/4 time

BALANCE
See *Foundations*, page 92.

A lyrical terre à terre movement set on a waltz rhythm in which the accent is on the first step.

BALANCE EN AVANT AND EN ARRIERE
En croisé, classical pose, right foot derrière; bras bas:

Commencing with a fondu on the supporting leg, the right foot begins to extend devant with a light sliding movement. The weight is transferred onto the right foot en fondu. The action allows the left foot to be released and brought momentarily to cou-de-pied derrière. The weight is then transferred first onto the half-pointe of the left foot and then back again onto the right foot en fondu. To repeat the action en arrière, the left leg extends derrière with a light sliding movement. The weight is transferred onto the left foot en fondu, allowing the right foot to be released and brought momentarily to cou-de-pied derrière. The weight is then transferred first onto the half-pointe of the right foot and then back again onto the left foot en fondu.

The arms move directly to a high 1st arabesque line for the balancé en avant and move directly to 3rd position for the balancé en arrière with the eyes following the track of the front arm.

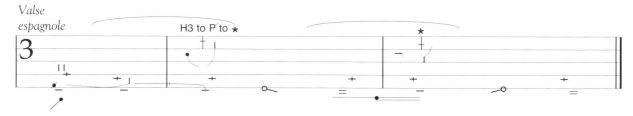

Balancé en avant and en arrière in 3/4 time

BALLONNE COMPOSE

See *Foundations*, page 85.

A composite step consisting of a ballonné, a posé, and a close to 5th position.

BALLONNE COMPOSE EN AVANT

En face, 5th position right foot devant; bras bas:

The movement commences with a demi-plié: as the knees bend, the right foot begins to slide forward. The combination of the sliding movement and the push-off from the supporting leg provides the force to spring into the air, extending the right leg to 45 degrees at the height of the jump. This movement travels forward. Maintaining the height of the right thigh, the knee bends and the foot is brought in to contact the middle of the shin of the supporting leg on landing. The action continues with a posé forward onto the right foot into dégagé derrière and is completed with a close to 5th position derrière.

The movement may also be taken en arrière and de côté with various arm positions.

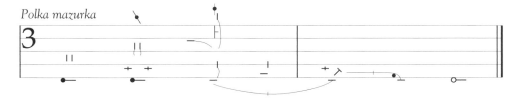

Polka mazurka

Ballonné composé in 3/4 time

BATTERIE

See *Foundations*, page 98.

ENTRECHAT TROIS

A beaten jump in which the legs perform three actions.

ENTRECHAT TROIS DERRIERE

En face, 5th position right foot devant; bras bas:

On leaving the ground, the legs open slightly sideways in order to execute the beating action with the right leg devant. The right foot then passes to finish sur le cou-de-pied derrière on landing.

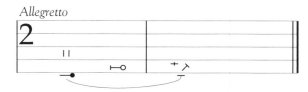

Allegretto

Entrechat trois derrière in 2/4 time

ENTRECHAT TROIS DEVANT

En face, 5th position right foot derrière; bras bas:

On leaving the ground, the legs open slightly sideways in order to execute the beating action with the right leg derrière. The right foot then passes to finish sur le cou-de-pied devant on landing.

Allegretto

Entrechat trois devant in 2/4 time

ENTRECHAT CINQ

A beaten jump in which the legs perform five actions.

ENTRECHAT CINQ DERRIERE

En face, 5th position right foot devant; bras bas:

On leaving the ground, the legs open slightly sideways in order to execute the beating action with the left leg devant. The left foot then passes to finish sur le cou-de-pied derrière on landing.

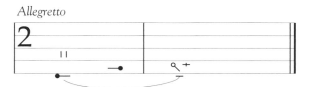

Allegretto

Entrechat cinq derrière in 2/4 time

ENTRECHAT CINQ DEVANT

En face, 5th position right foot derrière; bras bas:

On leaving the ground, the legs open slightly sideways in order to execute the beating action with the right leg devant. The left foot then passes to finish sur le cou-de-pied devant on landing.

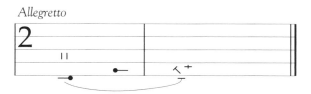

Allegretto

Entrechat cinq devant in 2/4 time

ENTRECHAT SIX

A beaten jump in which the legs perform six actions.

En face, 5th position right foot devant; bras bas:

On leaving the ground, the legs open slightly sideways in order to execute the beating action with the left leg devant. The legs reopen and beat with the right leg devant and then pass to land in 5th position with the left foot devant.

This movement requires sufficiently high elevation to ensure that the first two beating actions are executed on the spring upwards.

Allegretto

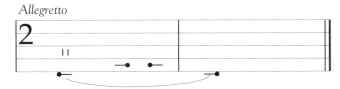

Entrechat six in 2/4 time

ECHAPPE SAUTE BATTU TO 2ND POSITION

See *Foundations*, page 81.

An échappé sauté to 2nd position with a beating action of the legs.

En face, 5th position right foot devant; bras bas:

On leaving the ground, the legs open slightly sideways in order to execute the beating action with the left leg devant before landing in 2nd position.

The movement may also incorporate two beats, with the left leg devant then derrière, before landing in 2nd position.

Moderato

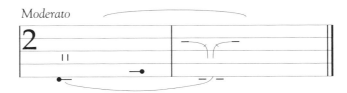

Échappé sauté battu to 2nd position in 2/4 time

ECHAPPE SAUTE BATTU FERME WITH THE BEAT OF AN ENTRECHAT SIX

An échappé sauté to 2nd position, returning to 5th position with a beating action of the legs.

En face, 5th position right foot devant; bras bas:

The first action is an échappé sauté to 2nd position. On the inward action, the legs beat with the left leg devant, open slightly sideways before beating with the right leg devant and then pass to land in 5th position en demi-plié with the left foot devant.

This may also be taken beating the legs with the left leg devant then derrière before landing in 2nd position, and without a change of feet on the inward action.

This movement is usually taken with a basic port de bras.

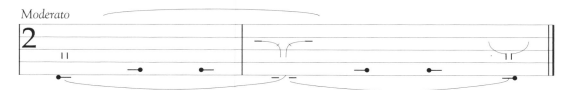

Échappé sauté battu to 2nd position with the beat of an entrechat six on the opening and closing in 2/4 time

ENTRECHAT SIX DE VOLEE DE COTE

An assemblé dessus de côté incorporating the beat of an entrechat six.

En croisé, left foot dégagé derrière; bras bas; head to 1:

The movement commences with a demi-contretemps to face 6, raising the arms to 1st position. The right foot then begins to slide toward 2nd position and the strong push-off from the supporting leg provides the force to spring into the air, travelling sideways and facing 5, beating the legs fully stretched in 5th position with the right leg devant. The legs open slightly sideways in order to execute the beating action with the left leg devant and then pass to land with the right foot devant in 5th position en demi-plié. Co-ordinating with the push-off and assisting the flight through the air, the arms move from 1st to open 4th position with the eye focus to the raised right arm. The arm position is held on landing.

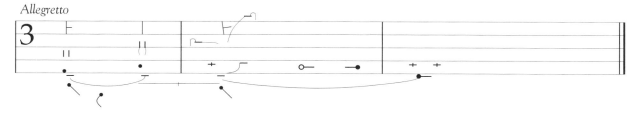

Entrechat six de volée de côté in 3/4 time

BRISE

See *Foundations*, page 99.

A travelling beaten step.

BRISE EN AVANT

En face, 5th position right foot devant; bras bas:

As the demi-plié commences, the right foot begins to slide toward 4th position devant at glissé height. The combination of the sliding movement and the push-off from the supporting leg provides the force to spring into the air, bringing the supporting leg up to the extended leg to beat derrière before changing to land in 5th position with the left foot devant.

Brisés may also be taken en arrière, and de côté devant or derrière. In brisé devant and derrière the foot slides toward 2nd position and the movement travels sideways to finish with a change of feet. In brisé devant, the front foot extends and the supporting foot joins it to beat derrière. In brisé derrière, the back foot extends and the supporting foot joins it to beat devant.

With the exception of brisé volé, the starting or finishing positions for all brisés may be 5th position, or sur le cou-de-pied devant or derrière, with various arm positions. When taken from cou-de-pied, the foot passes through 5th position in order to execute the sliding action.

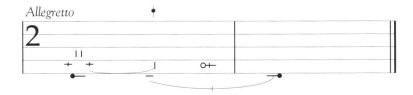

Brisé en avant in 2/4 time

BRISE VOLE DEVANT AND DERRIERE

En croisé, right foot dégagé derrière; arms 2nd position; head to 1:

From dégagé derrière the right foot brushes through 1st position en demi-plié toward 4th position devant at 45 degrees and the arms move through bras bas toward 1st position. The combination of the sliding movement, the push-off from the left leg, and co-ordinated use of the arms provides the force to spring into the air. The supporting leg is brought up to the extended leg and beats derrière before changing to land in 4th position devant at 45 degrees en fondu with the arms in 1st position, the body inclined toward the supporting leg, and the head inclined, turned and lowered over the right forearm. The left leg then brushes through 1st position en demi-plié toward 45 degrees derrière and the arms open, moving toward demi-seconde. The right leg is brought up to the extended leg and beats devant before changing to land in 4th position derrière at 45 degrees en fondu with the arms in an elongated demi-seconde position slightly behind the body and the head to 1. Heightened awareness of the opening of the chest and use of the upper back cause a slight inclination of the upper body to the left.

Brisé volé derrière may be taken with a rond de jambe action en dehors replacing the brush through 1st position.

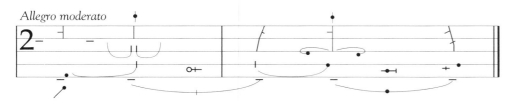

Brisé volé devant and derrière in 2/4 time

COUPE BRISE

A composite step incorporating a coupé action and a brisé from one leg to the other.

COUPE BRISE DERRIERE

En croisé, classical pose, right foot derrière; bras bas; head to 1:

The movement commences with a fondu on the supporting leg. As the right leg makes a coupé dessous, the left foot begins to slide toward 4th position derrière at glissé height. The combination of the sliding movement and the push-off from the supporting leg provides the force to spring into the air, bringing the supporting leg up to the extended leg to beat devant before changing to land on the left leg with the right foot sur le cou-de-pied derrière.

The brisé travels en arrière.

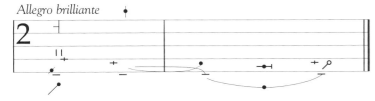

Coupé brisé derrière in 2/4 time

COUPE BRISE DEVANT

En croisé, right foot sur le cou-de-pied devant en fondu; bras bas; head to 1:

As the right leg makes a coupé dessus, the left foot begins to slide toward 4th position devant at glissé height. The combination of the sliding movement and the push-off from the supporting leg provides the force to spring into the air, bringing the supporting leg up to the extended leg to beat derrière before changing to land on the left leg with the right foot sur le cou-de-pied devant.

The brisé travels en avant.

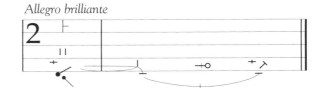

Coupé brisé devant in 2/4 time

BALLOTTE SAUTE

A rocking movement in which the weight is transferred by jumping from one foot to the other.

BALLOTTE SAUTE DESSOUS AND DESSUS

Facing 6, left leg 4th position derrière en l'air at 45 degrees en fondu; arms 3rd position right arm forward; eye focus over the right forearm:

With a strong push into the air from the supporting leg, the knees bend and the feet are drawn up to stretch fully in 5th position at the height of the ballotté dessous. The upper body inclines slightly backward as the right leg unfolds to land in 4th position devant en fondu. The right arm opens toward 2nd position as the left arm moves toward 1st position at the height of the jump, and the arms arrive in 3rd position with the left arm forward and the head to 1 on the landing.

With a strong push into the air from the supporting leg, the knees bend and the feet are drawn up to stretch fully in 5th position at the height of the ballotté dessus. There is a slight forward inclination of the body as the left leg unfolds to land in 4th position derrière en fondu. The left arm opens toward 2nd position as the right arm moves toward 1st position at the height of the jump, and the arms arrive in 3rd position with the right arm forward and the eye focus over the right forearm on the landing.

The degree of bend in the knees at the height of the jump is equivalent to the degree of bend when one foot is at mid-shin height. See *Foundations*, page 15.

The inclination of the upper body comes from the thoracic spine, with the pelvis and lumbar spine securely held.

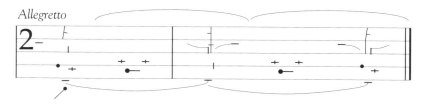

Ballotté sauté dessous and dessus in 2/4 time

CABRIOLE

An allegro step incorporating a single or double beating action of the legs in 4th position devant or derrière, or in 2nd position.

CABRIOLE OUVERTE DEVANT

En croisé, 4th position left leg devant; arms 2nd position:

From a demi-plié in 4th position and with a strong push off the left leg, the right leg brushes through 1st position into a battement to 4th position devant and is immediately followed by the left leg, which beats under the right causing it to rebound upwards to 90 degrees. The movement ends in effacé devant en l'air en fondu.

The arms move through bras bas and 1st position on the brushing action to arrive in effacé devant at the height of the jump.

Strong use of the abdominal muscles is necessary to support the trunk, facilitate the powerful use of the legs, and sustain the position in the air and on landing.

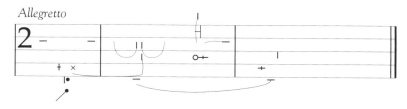

Cabriole ouverte devant in 2/4 time

CABRIOLE OUVERTE DERRIERE

En croisé, 4th position left leg devant; arms 2nd position:

From a demi-plié in 4th position and with a strong push off the right leg, the left leg brushes through 1st position into a battement to 4th position derrière and is immediately followed by the right leg, which beats under the left causing it to rebound upwards to 90 degrees. The movement ends in 1st arabesque en fondu.

The arms move through bras bas and 1st position on the brushing action to arrive in 1st arabesque at the height of the jump.

Allegro moderato

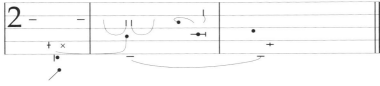

Cabriole ouverte derrière in 2/4 time

CABRIOLE OUVERTE DE COTE

En face, 5th position right leg devant; bras bas:

From a demi-plié in 5th position and with a strong push off the left leg, the right leg brushes to 2nd position with a battement action and is immediately followed by the left leg, which beats behind the right leg causing it to rebound upwards to 90 degrees. The movement ends in 2nd position en l'air en fondu.

The body inclines slightly to the left as the right leg brushes to 2nd position. The arms move through 1st position to arrive in 2nd position at the height of the jump, and the inclination is sustained on landing.

Cabriole ouverte de côté may also be taken with the back leg performing the battement action and the other leg beating in front.

Allegro moderato

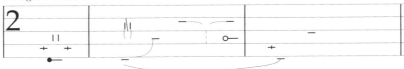

Cabriole ouverte de côté commencing with the front leg in 2/4 time

Allegro moderato

Cabriole ouverte de côté commencing with the back leg in 2/4 time

CABRIOLE FERMEE DEVANT

En croisé, 4th position left leg devant; arms 2nd position:

The action is the same as for cabriole ouverte devant, with the right leg closing to 5th position devant en demi-plié immediately after landing on the left leg, retaining the effacé devant line.

Grande valse

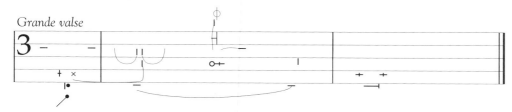

Cabriole fermée devant in 3/4 time

CABRIOLE FERMEE DERRIERE

En croisé, 4th position left leg devant; arms 2nd position:

The action is the same as for cabriole ouverte derrière, with the left leg closing to 5th position derrière en demi-plié immediately after landing on the right leg. The arms are retained in the 1st arabesque line.

Grande valse

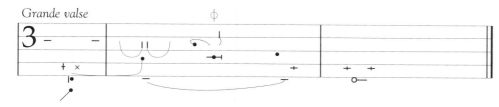

Cabriole fermée derrière in 3/4 time

CABRIOLE FERMEE DE COTE DEVANT

En face, 5th position right leg devant; bras bas:

The action is the same as for cabriole ouverte de côté devant, with the right leg closing to 5th position devant or derrière en demi-plié immediately after landing on the left leg. The arms and inclination of the body are retained.

This movement may be executed commencing with the right leg derrière, beating the left leg behind before closing in 5th position with the right leg devant.

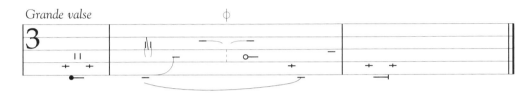

Cabriole fermée de côté devant in 3/4 time

CABRIOLE FERMEE DE COTE DERRIERE

En face, 5th position right leg derrière; bras bas:

The action is the same as for cabriole ouverte de côté derrière, with the right leg closing to 5th position derrière or devant en demi-plié immediately after landing on the left leg. The arms and inclination of the body are retained.

This movement may be executed commencing with the right leg devant, beating the left leg in front before closing to 5th position with the right leg derrière.

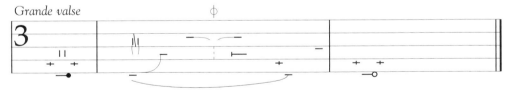

Cabriole fermée de côté derrière in 3/4 time

FAILLI

A composite step consisting of a jump from two feet to one, leading into a chassé passé.

En croisé, 5th position right foot devant; bras bas; head to 1:

As the jump commences, the legs join in a soubresaut position and the body turns to 6. The position is held until the left leg is released to arabesque just below 45 degrees a moment before landing. The movement finishes with a chassé passé to 6.

The arms move to 1st position on the chassé passé and the head remains to 1 throughout.

The jump is taken on the anacrusis and the chassé passé on the beat.

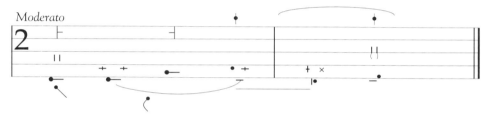

Failli in 2/4 time

COUPE FOUETTE RACCOURCI SAUTE

A coupé action leading into a vertical jump with an inward whipping action of the working leg.

En face, left foot sur le cou-de-pied derrière en fondu; arms 3rd position right arm forward; eye focus over the right forearm:

From a coupé action of the left foot and a strong vertical push into the air, the right leg extends to 2nd position at 45 degrees before making an inward whipping action that finishes mid-calf height derrière on landing.

The right arm moves to 2nd position with the outward action of the right leg, head to 1, and the left arm moves across to 3rd position on the inward action, with the eye focus over the left forearm.

This movement may be executed en tournant, with a 1/2-turn on the coupé and outward leg action.

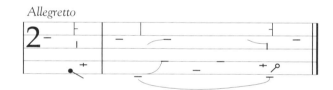

Coupé fouetté raccourci sauté in 2/4 time

FOUETTE SAUTE

A vertical jump with a turning action of the body away from the raised leg.

Facing 2, left foot dégagé devant; arms 2nd position:

From a demi-plié in 4th position and with a strong push off the left leg, the right leg brushes through 1st position into a battement to 4th position devant as the arms pass through bras bas and 1st to 5th position. The hips rotate to enable the right leg to pass through 2nd position en face and adjust behind the hip into 1st arabesque facing 4. The arms remain in 5th position when the leg passes through 2nd position and open to 1st arabesque on the final quarter of the turn. The strong turn of the head from 2 to 4 is co-ordinated with the fouetté action. The height of the leg is retained throughout and the movement finishes in 1st arabesque en fondu facing 4.

The strong fouetté action and 1/2-turn of the torso occur with a lift in the upper body and through use of both sides of the trunk, especially the muscles on the side of the raised leg. Engaging the gluteal muscles on the left side ensures and reinforces the turnout of the left leg as the pelvis rotates.

This movement may be executed with a 1/2-turn from corner to corner finishing in either 1st or 2nd arabesque.

When taken on a 3/4 rhythm, the battement action occurs on the first beat of the first bar and the landing on the first beat of the second bar.

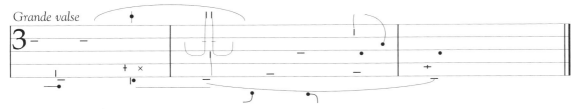

Fouetté sauté in 3/4 time

FOUETTE SAUTE BATTU

The action is the same as for fouetté sauté, with the left leg beating under the right at the height of the jump in 4th position devant facing 2.

This movement may be executed with a 1/2-turn from corner to corner finishing in either 1st or 2nd arabesque.

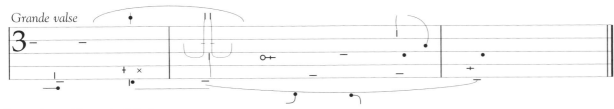

Fouetté sauté battu in 3/4 time

GRAND FOUETTE SAUTE EN TOURNANT

A composite step consisting of a grand battement sauté in 2nd position and a fouetté sauté with a 1/2-turn from corner to corner.

En croisé, right foot dégagé derrière; bras bas; head to 1:

From dégagé derrière and with a strong push off the left leg, the right leg brushes through 1st position en demi-plié into a battement sauté to 2nd position at 90 degrees while the body turns to face 5 and the arms move through 1st to 2nd position with the head to 6.

The height of the leg is retained on landing. The movement continues with a swivelling action to face 8 and, with a strong push off the left leg, the right leg brushes through 1st position en demi-plié into a battement to 4th position devant. The arms move through 1st to 5th position with the eye focus to 8. The movement finishes with a fouetté sauté landing in 2nd arabesque facing 6 with the head and eye focus to 6.

This action may also be executed with the beating action of a fouetté sauté battu.

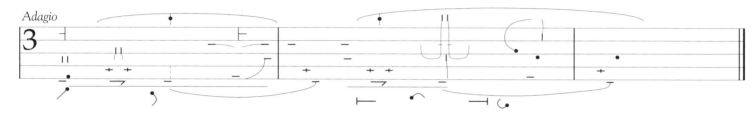

Grand fouetté sauté en tournant in 3/4 time

GARGOUILLADE

A light spring from one foot to the other, incorporating the action of a double rond de jambe en l'air.

En face, 5th position right foot devant; arms 3rd position right arm forward; head to 6:

From a demi-plié, the right foot is released so that the lower leg is vertical and leads into a spring upwards. The right leg executes the circling action of a double rond de jambe en l'air en dehors before opening slightly in preparation for landing. The left leg immediately follows the right leg and, at the height of the jump, executes the circling action of a single rond de jambe en l'air en dedans and an additional inward circling action before passing through retiré devant and closing in 5th position devant en demi-plié.

The arms are held in 3rd position throughout, with the eye line over the forearm to 6.

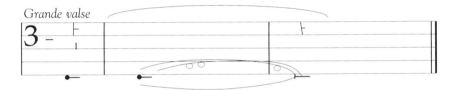

Grande valse

Gargouillade in 3/4 time

GARGOUILLADE FINISHING IN DEGAGE DEVANT

En face, 5th position right foot devant; arms 2nd position:

From a demi-plié, the left foot is released so that the lower leg is vertical and leads into a spring upwards. The left leg executes the circling action of a double rond de jambe en l'air en dedans. At the height of the jump the left leg is immediately followed by the right, which executes the action of a développé passé. The movement finishes in dégagé devant en fondu on the left leg facing 6.

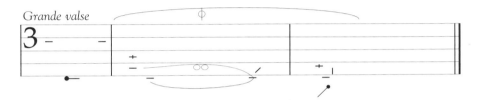

Grande valse

Gargouillade finishing in dégagé devant in 3/4 time

PAS DE BOURREE

See *Foundations*, page 86.

PAS DE BOURREE EN AVANT

A pas de bourrée travelling forward.

En face, 5th position right foot devant; bras bas:

From a demi-plié, the left foot extends to 4th position derrière at glissé height, and then closes into 5th position derrière en demi-pointes; the right foot immediately steps forward to a small 4th position en demi-pointes, then the left foot closes into 5th position derrière en demi-plié.

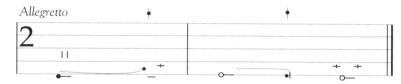

Pas de bourrée en avant in 2/4 time

PAS DE BOURREE EN ARRIERE

A pas de bourrée travelling backward.

En face, 5th position right foot devant; bras bas:

From a demi-plié, the right foot extends to 4th position devant at glissé height, and then closes into 5th position devant en demi-pointes; the left foot immediately steps back to a small 4th position en demi-pointes, then the right foot closes into 5th position devant en demi-plié.

Pas de bourrée en arrière in 2/4 time

PAS DE BOURREE COURU EN AVANT

En face, 5th position right foot devant; bras bas:

From a demi-plié, the right foot extends to 4th position devant at glissé height and steps into 4th position en demi-pointes; the left foot immediately closes into 5th position derrière en demi-pointes, then the right foot is released to transfer the weight forward into 4th position en demi-plié.

A variation of this, the running pas de bourrée, is the step-run-step action used to generate momentum, often leading into travelled grand allegro actions.

Pas de bourrée couru en avant may be taken omitting the final demi-plié in 4th position and ending in a dégagé devant en fondu.

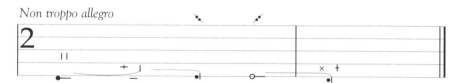

Pas de bourrée couru en avant in 6/8 time

PAS DE BOURREE COURU EN ARRIERE

En face, 5th position right foot devant; bras bas:

From a demi-plié, the left foot extends to 4th position derrière at glissé height and steps into 4th position en demi-pointes; the right foot immediately closes into 5th position devant en demi-pointes, then the left foot is released to transfer the weight backward into 4th position en demi-plié.

Pas de bourrée couru en arrière may be taken omitting the final demi-plié in 4th position and ending in a dégagé derrière en fondu.

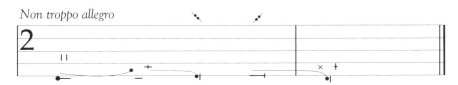

Pas de bourrée couru en arrière in 6/8 time

PAS DE BOURREE COURU DE COTE DEVANT

En face, 5th position right foot devant; bras bas:

From a demi-plié, the right foot extends to 2nd position at glissé height and steps into 2nd position en demi-pointes; the left foot immediately closes to 5th position derrière en demi-pointes, then the right foot is released to transfer the weight sideways into 2nd position en demi-plié.

Pas de bourrée couru de côté derrière is taken with the action of a pas de bourrée derrière.

Pas de bourrée couru de côté devant and derrière may be taken omitting the final demi-plié in 2nd position and ending in a dégagé to 2nd position en fondu.

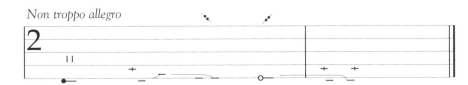

Pas de bourrée couru de côté devant in 6/8 time

PAS DE BOURREE EN TOURNANT

A pas de bourrée taken sur place, incorporating a turning action.

PAS DE BOURREE DESSUS EN TOURNANT

En face, 5th position right foot devant; bras bas:

From a demi-plié, the left foot extends to 4th position derrière at glissé height and, with a swivelling action on the right foot, executes a rond de jambe en dedans with a 1/4-turn, closing in 5th position devant en demi-pointes facing 2. Continuing with a 1/2-turn to the right, the right foot immediately steps to a small 2nd position en demi-pointes. The left foot then closes into 5th position derrière en demi-plié to complete the final quarter of the turn.

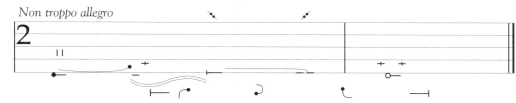

Pas de bourrée dessus en tournant in 6/8 time

PAS DE BOURREE DESSOUS EN TOURNANT

En face, 5th position right foot devant; bras bas:

From a demi-plié, the right foot extends to 4th position devant at glissé height and, with a swivelling action on the left foot, executes a rond de jambe en dehors with a 1/4-turn closing in 5th position derrière en demi-pointes facing 2. Continuing with a 1/2-turn to the right, the left foot immediately steps to a small 2nd position en demi-pointes. The right foot then closes into 5th position devant en demi-plié to complete the final quarter of the turn.

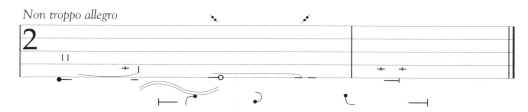

Pas de bourrée dessous en tournant in 6/8 time

JETE ORDINAIRE

See *Foundations*, page 82.

A jump that takes off from one leg and lands on the other.

JETE ORDINAIRE EN AVANT

En face, 5th position right foot devant; bras bas:

From the demi-plié, the right leg slides to 4th position devant just below 45 degrees, co-ordinating with a spring off the supporting leg. The combination of the sliding action and the strong push off the supporting leg provides the force to travel forward. The left leg comes in behind the right leg with the big toe contacting the base of the calf on landing.

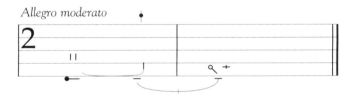

Jeté ordinaire en avant in 2/4 time

JETE ORDINAIRE EN ARRIERE

The action is the same as for jeté ordinaire en avant except the movement travels backward. The finishing position is with the little toe in contact at mid-shin height devant.

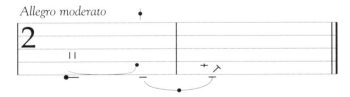

Jeté ordinaire en arrière in 2/4 time

JETE ORDINAIRE DE COTE

The action is the same as for jeté ordinaire devant and derrière except that the movement travels sideways.

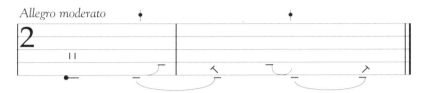

Jeté ordinaire de côté devant to the right and left in 2/4 time

JETE BATTEMENT

A jeté ordinaire taken terre à terre incorporating the beating action of a double battement frappé. This movement develops speed and dexterity of footwork.

JETE BATTEMENT EN AVANT

En face, right leg in 2nd position at glissé height en fondu; bras bas with use of épaulement:

Completing a small vertical spring onto the right foot, the left foot immediately flexes in order to execute a double battement frappé that beats derrière-devant. The fondu is retained throughout the beating action and extension.

The use of épaulement co-ordinates with the extension to 2nd position, with the left shoulder forward over the extended leg.

This may also be taken en arrière with the double battement frappé beating devant-derrière, and with use of épaulement over the supporting leg.

When taken on a 2/4 rhythm the battement frappé action is executed on the counts "& a" and the final extension is completed on the first beat of the bar.

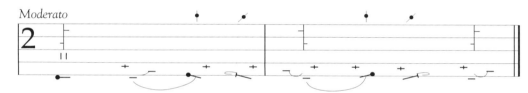

Jeté battement en avant in 2/4 time

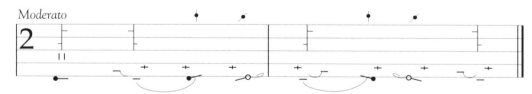

Jeté battement en arrière in 2/4 time

JETE PASSE

A jump from one open position to another with the legs passing each other at the height of the jump.

JETE PASSE DERRIERE IN ATTITUDE

En face, right leg attitude derrière at 90 degrees with the toes centred behind the body en fondu; bras bas:

From a strong push off the supporting leg, the left leg passes the right at the height of the jump before landing in attitude derrière.

Strong use of the back extensors holds the shoulders open, facilitates the powerful action of the legs, and sustains the position on landing.

This movement may also be taken with the legs in attitude devant or with straight legs devant or derrière.

When taken on a 3/4 rhythm, the jump is suspended through the 2nd and 3rd beats of the bar.

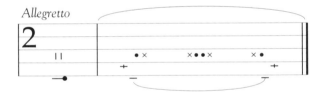

Allegretto

Jeté passé derrière in attitude in 2/4 time

GRAND JETE EN AVANT WITH DEVELOPPE

See *Foundations*, page 96.

A large leap from one foot to the other travelling forward, initiated with a développé action.

En croisé, left foot dégagé devant; arms 2nd position:

The preparation for the jump consists of a step forward on the left foot into 4th position en demi-plié which acts as a springboard for the jump. Co-ordinated with a strong push-off and développé passé into 4th position devant, the 3rd arabesque line is established as soon as possible. There is maximum extension of both legs at the height of the jump and a sense of suspension during the flight forward. After landing on the right leg, the movement continues with a chassé passé.

The arms pass in a continuous movement through bras bas and 1st position to arrive in 3rd arabesque at the height of the jump, with the eye line projected to 6.

Grande valse

Grand jeté en avant with développé in 3/4 time

JETE ELANCE EN TOURNANT

A composite step consisting of a grand jeté en avant incorporating a swift, darting quality, and a turning action.

JETE ELANCE WITH A COUPE ACTION EN TOURNANT

Facing 2, right foot sur le cou-de-pied devant en fondu; arms 1st position:

From a strong push off the left leg, the right leg is thrown to 4th position devant en l'air at 90 degrees directly into the line of travel. The 1st arabesque line is established as soon as possible, with the front arm slightly above shoulder level and the legs fully extended at the height of the jump. The 1st arabesque position is retained on landing. The turn to the right then occurs by a coupé dessous, with the left leg immediately drawn under the body and the right releasing to finish sur le cou-de-pied devant en fondu facing 2.

To facilitate the turn, the arms move directly from 1st arabesque to 1st position, with the head and eye focus used as for a pirouette. To assist the projection forward and enhance the élancé quality, the sides of the waist must be evenly lengthened and the shoulder line squared.

This movement is usually taken in a series en diagonale or en manège.

Jeté élancé with a coupé action en tournant in 2/4 time

JETE ELANCE WITH PAS DE BOURREE DESSUS EN TOURNANT

This movement is performed as jeté élancé with a coupé action en tournant, but with the turn occurring by a swift pas de bourrée dessus en tournant. When taken in series, the third action of the pas de bourrée is a coupé dessous.

Facing 2, 5th position right foot devant; arms 1st position:

From a demi-plié, the right leg executes a battement action to 4th position devant en l'air and there is a strong push off the left leg into the jump. The 1st arabesque line, with the front arm slightly above shoulder level, is established as soon as possible with the legs fully extended at the height of the jump. The 1st arabesque position is retained on landing. As the turn to the right occurs, the movement continues with a swift pas de bourrée dessus en tournant commencing with the left leg, finishing facing 2.

The arms move directly from 1st arabesque to 1st position, with the head and eye focus used as for a pirouette.

A square shoulder line, with the sides of the waist evenly lengthened, assists the projection forward and the élancé quality.

This movement is usually taken in a series en diagonale or en manège.

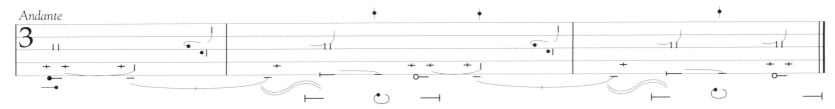

Jeté élancé with pas de bourrée dessus en tournant in 3/4 time

GRAND JETE

GRAND JETE EN TOURNANT IN ATTITUDE

A grand allegro step in which the legs and body trace an arc shape through the air.

Facing 6, left foot sur le cou-de-pied derrière en fondu; bras bas:

From a coupé dessous making a 1/4-turn to the right, there is a strong push off the left leg into the jump as the right is thrown directly to 4th position devant en l'air. The arms pass through 1st position on the coupé and open to 4th position with the left arm raised on the push-off, establishing the attitude derrière position as soon as possible. The strong lift of the leg, arms, and torso, co-ordinated with the jumping action, traces an arc in the air as the movement travels forward, as if travelling along a curved path from 7 to 5, with the height of the jump achieved as the body passes 8. This is assisted by use of the head and eye focus from 6 to 1. The attitude derrière position is sustained on landing.

When this movement is taken en manège, each jeté lands facing the direction of travel, sustaining the attitude derrière position. Each is linked with a coupé dessous en tournant making a 1/2-turn.

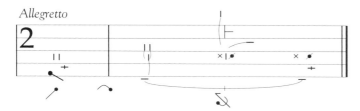

Grand jeté en tournant in attitude in 2/4 time

GRAND JETE EN TOURNANT

A vertical jump with a 1/2-turn in the air.

Facing 6, left foot dégagé derrière; arms 2nd position:

The preparation consists of three runs toward corner 8, with the dancer gradually turning to face that corner as the arms pass in a continuous movement through bras bas and 1st position. The head turns to 8 on the second step. The third step which is shorter, assisted by the impetus of the arms preparing to take 5th position, acts as a springboard for the vertical jump as the right leg makes a battement into 4th position devant en l'air. With a strong 1/2-turn of the body, the legs pass in the air at the height of the jump. The arms are retained in 5th position before opening to 2nd position on the landing in 4th position derrière en l'air en fondu, head to 6.

The stronger the push-off from the third step, the higher the jump.

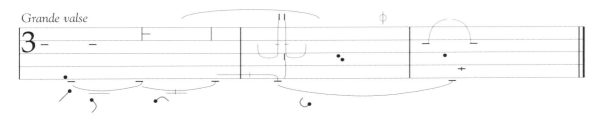

Grand jeté en tournant prepared by runs in 3/4 time

GRAND JETE BATTU EN TOURNANT

The action is the same as for grand jeté en tournant, but incorporates a beating action.

After the right leg makes the battement into 4th position devant en l'air and the body begins to rotate, the left leg lifts to beat in front of the right before the legs pass at the height of the jump.

Grand jeté battu en tournant prepared by runs in 3/4 time

GRAND PAS DE BASQUE EN TOURNANT

See *Foundations*, page 91.

A grand allegro step incorporating a large pas de basque and a pas de bourrée dessus en tournant.

En croisé, 5th position right foot devant; bras bas; head and eye focus to 1 throughout:

From a demi-plié, leading into a spring turning toward 6, the right leg extends and executes a circular movement en dehors to 90 degrees passing half-way between 4th position devant and 2nd position. The left leg immediately lifts to half-way between 2nd and 4th position devant and makes a circular movement en dedans to reach 4th position devant en l'air at 90 degrees as the right leg lands en fondu. The arms co-ordinate with the action of the legs, moving through 1st to 5th position at the height of the jump and opening to 2nd position on landing.

The movement continues with a pas de bourrée dessus en tournant to finish facing 5 with the arms lowering to bras bas.

When taken on a 2/4 rhythm, the pas de basque is completed on the first beat of the bar and the pas de bourrée en tournant on the second beat of the bar.

Non troppo allegro

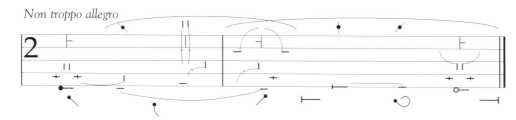

Grand pas de basque en tournant in 2/4 time

SAUT DE BASQUE

A grand allegro step incorporating a turning action at the height of the jump.

En croisé, right foot dégagé devant; arms 2nd position; head to 6:

From a step onto the right leg en fondu facing 6, the left leg brushes through 1st position and, with a 1/4-turn en dedans, continues into a battement in 2nd position pushing vertically into the air. The arms move through bras bas and 1st position to arrive in 5th position on the battement action. At the height of the jump as the turn continues, the left leg moves immediately under the body and the right lifts directly to retiré devant. The position of the arms is sustained on landing in retiré devant en fondu facing 5.

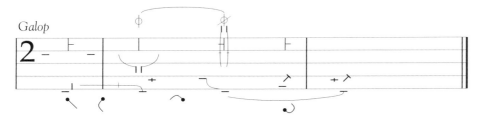

Saut de basque in 2/4 time

GRAND ROND DE JAMBE EN L'AIR SAUTE AND PAS DE BOURREE DESSOUS EN TOURNANT WITH A RENVERSE ACTION

En croisé, right leg sur le cou-de-pied derrière en fondu; arms 3rd position left arm forward:

From a coupé dessous, the right arm moves through bras bas and 1st position as the left leg extends forward into grand rond de jambe sauté to 4th position derrière at 90 degrees, landing en fondu facing 5. The arms move through 5th position as the leg passes through 2nd position en face and reach 2nd position as the leg arrives in 4th position derrière with the chest open and the head turned to 1. The renversé action is co-ordinated with the pas de bourrée dessous en tournant to finish facing 6.

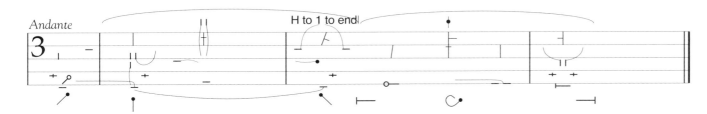

Grand rond de jambe en l'air sauté and pas de bourrée dessous en tournant with a renversé action in 3/4 time

RETIRE SAUTE

See *Foundations*, page 42.

A vertical jump incorporating a retiré action.

Retiré sauté may be taken with the working leg lifted devant or derrière to petit retiré or retiré position.

RETIRE SAUTE DEVANT

En face, 5th position right foot devant; bras bas:

The jump commences with a strong push-off from a demi-plié, and the right leg is immediately drawn up to retiré devant. The left leg is fully stretched under the body. The movement finishes in 5th position en demi-plié, right foot devant.

Retiré sauté devant in 2/4 time

RETIRE SAUTE DERRIERE

En face, 5th position right foot devant; bras bas:

The jump commences with a strong push-off from a demi-plié, and the left leg is immediately drawn up to retiré derrière. The right leg is fully stretched under the body. The movement finishes in 5th position en demi-plié, left foot derrière.

Retiré sauté derrière in 2/4 time

RETIRE SAUTE PASSE DERRIERE

The action is the same as for a retiré sauté devant, but from the retiré devant the working leg passes to finish derrière on landing.

Allegretto

Retiré sauté passé derrière in 2/4 time

RETIRE SAUTE PASSE DEVANT

The action of the leg is similar to retiré sauté derrière, but the working leg passes directly from 5th position derrière to retiré devant at the height of the jump before closing in 5th position devant en demi-plié.

Allegretto

Retiré sauté passé devant in 2/4 time

ROND DE JAMBE SAUTE

See *Foundations*, page 40.

A vertical jump incorporating the action of a rond de jambe en l'air at 45 degrees.

ROND DE JAMBE SAUTE EN DEHORS

En face, right leg 2nd position en l'air at 45 degrees; arms 2nd position:

From a strong push off the supporting leg, which then stretches fully under the body, the right leg executes a rond de jambe en l'air en dehors, with the final extension completed on landing en fondu.

This movement may incorporate the action of a single or double rond de jambe en dehors and may also be performed en dedans.

Allegretto

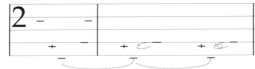

Single and double rond de jambe sauté en dehors in 2/4 time

Allegretto

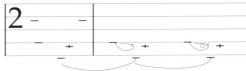

Single and double rond de jambe sauté en dedans in 2/4 time

92

SISSONNE FERMEE CHANGEE

See *Foundations*, page 94.

A sissonne fermée incorporating a change of feet.

SISSONNE FERMEE CHANGEE EN AVANT

En face, 5th position right foot devant; bras bas:

From a demi-plié, the jump travels forward with the left leg fully stretched under the body as the right leg passes to 4th position derrière at 45 degrees. After landing on the left leg, the right leg immediately closes to 5th position derrière en demi-plié.

The arms are taken through 1st position to demi-bras with the jump.

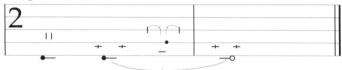

Allegro moderato

Sissonne fermée changée en avant in 2/4 time

SISSONNE FERMEE CHANGEE EN ARRIERE

En face, 5th position right foot devant; bras bas:

The action is the same as for sissonne fermée changée en avant, but the jump travels backward and the left leg passes to 4th position devant at 45 degrees before closing.

The arms are taken through 1st position to demi-bras with the jump.

Allegro moderato

Sissonne fermée changée en arrière in 2/4 time

SISSONNE OUVERTE

A travelling jump from two feet to one finishing in an open position en l'air.

SISSONNE OUVERTE EN AVANT

En face, 5th position right foot devant; bras bas:

From a demi-plié, the jump travels forward with the right leg fully stretched under the body as the left leg opens to 4th position derrière at 45 degrees. The 4th position en l'air is sustained on landing en fondu.

The arms are taken through 1st position to demi-bras with the jump.

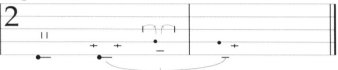

Allegro moderato

Sissonne ouverte en avant in 2/4 time

SISSONNE OUVERTE EN ARRIERE

En face, 5th position right foot devant; bras bas:

The action is the same as for sissonne ouverte en avant but the jump travels backward and the right leg opens to 4th position devant at 45 degrees.

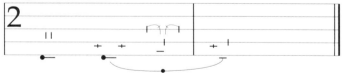

Allegro moderato

Sissonne ouverte en arrière in 2/4 time

SISSONNE OUVERTE DE COTE

En face, 5th position right foot devant; bras bas:

From a demi-plié, the jump travels sideways toward the back foot, with the left leg fully stretched under the body as the right leg opens to 2nd position at 45 degrees. The 2nd position en l'air is sustained on landing en fondu. The arms move through 1st to 2nd position with use of épaulement bringing the left shoulder forward.

Sissonne ouverte de côté may also be taken travelling sideways toward the front foot.

Allegro moderato

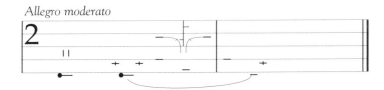

Sissonne ouverte de côté travelling toward the back foot in 2/4 time

Allegro moderato

Sissonne ouverte de côté travelling toward the front foot in 2/4 time

SISSONNE OUVERTE CHANGEE EN AVANT

En face, 5th position right foot devant; bras bas:

From a demi-plié, the jump travels forward with the left leg fully stretched under the body as the right leg passes to 4th position derrière at 45 degrees. The 4th position en l'air is sustained on landing. The arms are taken through 1st position to demi-bras with the jump.

Allegro moderato

Sissonne ouverte changée en avant in 2/4 time

SISSONNE OUVERTE CHANGEE EN ARRIERE

En face, 5th position right foot devant; bras bas:

The action is the same as for sissonne ouverte changée en avant but the jump travels backward and the left leg passes to 4th position devant at 45 degrees.

All sissonnes ouvertes may be taken with a développé action of the working leg.

Allegro moderato

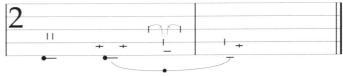

Sissonne ouverte changée en arrière in 2/4 time

SISSONNE BATTUE

When sissonnes are embellished with a beat, the action occurs before the working leg is released to its open position.

In sissonnes ouvertes and fermées en avant and en arrière, the legs change to beat.

In all other sissonnes ouvertes and fermées, there is no change of legs before the beating action.

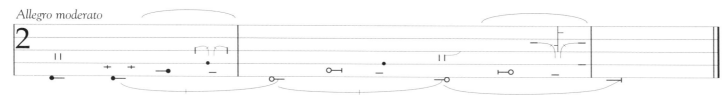

Sissonne battue fermée en avant, fermée changée en avant, and fermée de côté dessus in 2/4 time

SISSONNE DOUBLEE

A composite travelling step consisting of a sissonne ouverte, a coupé action, and an assemblé.
The coupé action transfers the weight under the body line without passing through cou-de-pied.

SISSONNE DOUBLEE DESSOUS
En face, 5th position right foot devant; bras bas:

The movement commences with a sissonne ouverte de côté travelling to the left, with the arms moving through 1st to 2nd position. There is a strong inclination of the body toward the supporting leg with use of épaulement. The movement continues with a coupé action dessous followed by an assemblé de côté dessous with use of épaulement, lowering the arms to bras bas on landing.

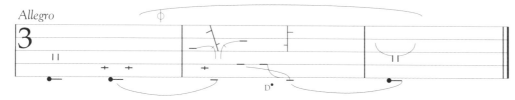

Sissonne doublée dessous in 3/4 time

SISSONNE DOUBLEE DESSUS

En face, 5th position right foot derrière; bras bas:

The movement commences with a sissonne ouverte de côté travelling to the left with the arms moving through 1st to 2nd position. There is a strong inclination of the body toward the supporting leg with use of épaulement. The movement continues with a coupé action dessus followed by an assemblé de côté dessus with use of épaulement, lowering the arms to bras bas on landing.

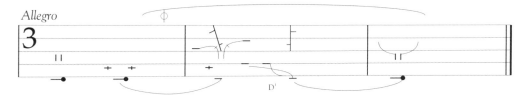

Sissonne doublée dessus in 3/4 time

SISSONNE DOUBLEE EN AVANT

This movement consists of a sissonne ouverte en avant, a coupé action dessous, and an assemblé en avant.

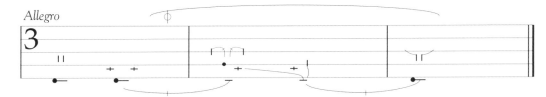

Sissonne doublée en avant in 3/4 time

SISSONNE DOUBLEE EN ARRIERE

This movement consists of a sissonne ouverte en arrière, a coupé action dessus, and an assemblé en arrière.

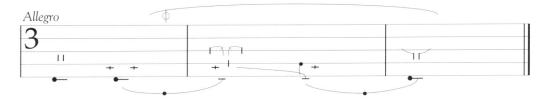

Sissonne doublée en arrière in 3/4 time

SISSONNE EN TOURNANT

A jump from two legs to one, incorporating a turn in the air.

En face, 5th position right foot devant; arms 3rd position right arm forward:

From the demi-plié, there is a strong push into the air and the right leg is immediately brought to its position sur le cou-de-pied devant. The impetus for the turn to the right comes from the combination of a strong push off both legs and the swift action of the incoming arm to 1st position. The position sur le cou-de-pied is sustained on landing en face.

This may be taken with the right foot commencing derrière and passing to cou-de-pied devant on the turning action.

Sissonne en tournant may incorporate a single or double turn in the air.

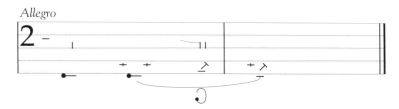

Sissonne en tournant in 2/4 time

SISSONNE OUVERTE CHANGEE EN TOURNANT IN ATTITUDE

En croisé, 5th position right foot devant; bras bas; head to 1:

From a demi-plié, there is a strong push-off into the jump, making 3/4-turn to the left, travelling forward toward 6. The left leg is fully stretched under the body as the right leg passes to attitude derrière, and the en l'air position is sustained on landing en fondu. The arms move through 1st to 4th position at the height of the jump with the eye focus to 1.

Strong use of the right side of the body assists the turning action and reinforces the squareness of the trunk.

This movement may also be taken into 2nd arabesque.

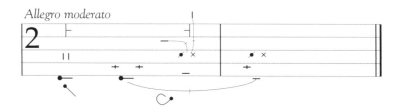

Sissonne ouverte changée en tournant in attitude in 2/4 time

TEMPS DE CUISSE

A composite terre à terre step consisting of a petit retiré or a battement glissé followed by a sissonne fermée.

TEMPS DE CUISSE DESSUS (FRENCH)

En face, 5th position right foot derrière; arms 3rd position right arm forward; head and eye focus over the forearm:

From a demi-plié and remaining en fondu, the right foot passes through petit retiré position and closes into 5th position devant en demi-plié. The movement continues with a sissonne fermée de côté devant.

When taken on a 2/4 rhythm, the petit retiré closes en demi-plié on the anacrusis and the sissonne fermée de côté closes on the first beat of the bar.

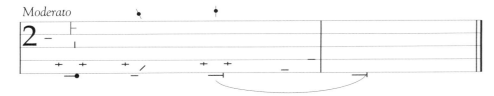

Temps de cuisse dessus (French) in 2/4 time

TEMPS DE CUISSE DESSOUS (FRENCH)

En face, 5th position right foot devant; arms 3rd position left arm forward; head and eye focus over the forearm:

From a demi-plié and remaining en fondu, the right foot passes through petit retiré position and closes into 5th position derrière en demplié. The movement continues with a sissonne fermée de côté derrière.

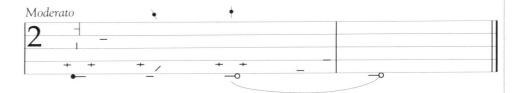

Temps de cuisse dessous (French) in 2/4 time

TEMPS DE CUISSE EN AVANT (FRENCH)

En face, 5th position right foot derrière; bras bas:

From a demi-plié and remaining en fondu, the right foot passes through petit retiré position and closes into 5th position devant en demi-plié. The movement continues with a sissonne fermée en avant.

Temps de cuisse may also be taken en arrière, commencing with the front foot, closing derrière, and ending with a sissonne fermée en arrière.

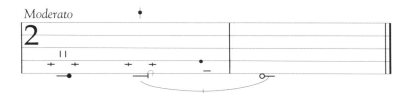

Temps de cuisse en avant (French) in 2/4 time

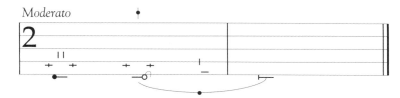

Temps de cuisse en arrière (French) in 2/4 time

TEMPS DE CUISSE DESSUS (ITALIAN)

En face, 5th position right foot derrière; arms 3rd position right arm forward; head and eye focus over the forearm:

From a demi-plié and remaining en fondu, the right foot extends to 2nd position at glissé height and closes into 5th position devant en demi-plié. The movement continues with a sissonne fermée de côté devant.

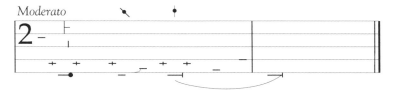

Temps de cuisse dessus (Italian) in 2/4 time

TEMPS DE CUISSE DESSOUS (ITALIAN)

En face, 5th position right foot devant; arms 3rd position left arm forward; head and eye focus over the forearm:

From a demi-plié and remaining en fondu, the right foot extends to 2nd position at glissé height and closes into 5th position derrière en demi-plié. The movement continues with a sissonne fermée de côté derrière.

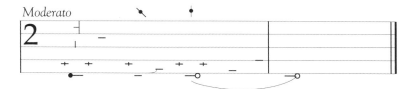

Temps de cuisse dessous (Italian) in 2/4 time

TEMPS DE CUISSE EN AVANT (ITALIAN)

En face, 5th position right foot derrière; bras bas:

From a demi-plié and remaining en fondu, the right foot extends to 2nd position at glissé height and closes into 5th position devant en demi-plié. The movement continues with a sissonne fermée en avant.

Temps de cuisse may also be taken en arrière, commencing with the front foot, closing derrière, and ending with a sissonne fermée en arrière.

Both French and Italian temps de cuisse may also be taken without a change of feet on the first action.

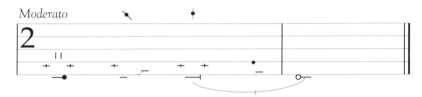

Temps de cuisse en avant (Italian) in 2/4 time

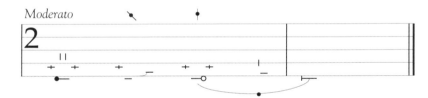

Temps de cuisse en arrière (Italian) in 2/4 time

TEMPS DE FLECHE

An allegro step with the first leg resembling the shape of a bow and the second foot tracing the path of an arrow.

Facing 6, left foot dégagé derrière; bras bas; head to 1:

The movement commences with a temps levé on the right leg with the left leg extended to 4th position derrière at 45 degrees. The left leg then brushes through 1st position en demi-plié into attitude devant at 90 degrees retaining the fondu, as the arms move to 1st position and the upper body inclines slightly to the right with the head and eye focus over the right forearm. The movement continues with a strong push-off and, as the dancer springs into the air, the right leg executes a développé passé to 4th position devant en l'air at 90 degrees. The extension is completed on the landing as the arms reach 5th position and the upper body inclines slightly to the left with the head and eye focus to 1. The right leg usually closes in 5th position devant en demi-plié with the arms opening to 2nd position.

When taken on a 3/4 rhythm, the temps levé is executed on the last two beats of the bar, the attitude is executed on the first beat of the next bar. The movement is completed on the first beat of the final bar.

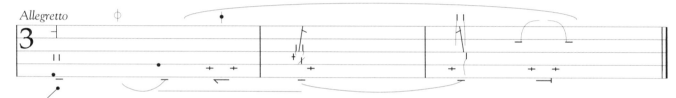

Temps de flèche in 3/4 time

TEMPS DE POISSON

A vertical jump of high elevation from two feet to one, with the body sustaining a curved line in the air.

En croisé, 5th position right foot devant; bras bas; head to 1:

From a demi-plié, there is a strong push-off into the jump, with the legs firmly held in 5th position and pulled slightly behind the body to create a curved line. The thoracic spine extends strongly as the body turns in the air to face 6 and the arms lift immediately through 1st to 5th position. The curved line of the body is sustained for as long as possible before landing on the right leg, with the arms in 5th position and the left leg in 4th position derrière at 45 degrees. The head and eye focus remain to 1 throughout.

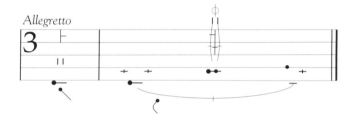

Temps de poisson in 3/4 time

DOUBLE TOUR EN L'AIR

See *Foundations*, page 97.

A changement en tournant incorporating two revolutions in the air.

En face, 5th position right foot devant; arms 3rd position right arm forward:

From a demi-plié, the right arm starts to move toward 2nd position. The force for the double turn to the right is achieved by the combination of both feet pushing off strongly into the air, the legs changing as soon as possible, and the left arm joining the right in 1st position. The eye focus is as described for a pirouette en dehors. The arms are held in 1st on landing in 5th position.

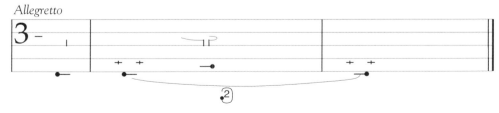

Double tour en l'air in 3/4 time

CONTENTS
CHAPTER SEVEN: POINTE WORK

CHAPTER SEVEN
POINTE WORK

When all the elements from barre to allegro come together in pointe work, how glorious it can look. Dancing en pointe, as epitomised by Odette's solo, *Swan Lake*, Act II, combines adagio and allegro movements of great virtuosity and great expressiveness, exquisitely linked to the music. Advanced pointe technique demands subtle gradations in the use of energy, just enough to achieve each movement seamlessly and effortlessly, with elegance and grace.

Not every female dancer can perform pointe work, even with the best instruction and the most sincere motivation. If a physique is not suited to the movements described in this chapter, it may be unsafe to attempt them. Attention to safe practice in pointe work begins with the careful selection and preparation of shoes[1]. They must fit the foot perfectly, complementing its line and allowing correct weight bearing. Ribbons must be sewn in exactly the right place to apply the force needed for ankle support and must be tied firmly but without constricting tendons and blood vessels. The knot should sit on the inside of the ankle in the soft depression behind the anklebone, so as not to apply pressure on the Achilles tendon. While some padding may be necessary, the sensitivity of the toes and ball of the foot should not be disturbed by anything too thick or constricting. A strong foot is in command of the shoe, not the other way around.

Safe dance practice in pointe work is reinforced through a slow build-up of perfectly placed basic work that strengthens the legs and feet. Building from the demi-pointe exercises introduced in *Foundations*, Chapter Two, the basic technique of rise and relevé onto pointe is described in *Foundations*, Chapter Eight. These exercises develop the intrinsic muscles of the foot, enhancing balance and proprioception on the flat foot and demi-pointe in preparation for pointe work. Since the full pointe position affords the dancer less friction than flat or demi-pointe, the dancer must also master the control of turnout at the hip before she attempts advanced pointe work. Poor alignment en pointe can seriously compromise the integrity of the legs and feet. Good control of the torso, correct weight placement, and proper alignment of the leg and foot joints in relation to the plumb-line lessen the harmful strain on body joints.

Once the dancer has mastered the rudiments of pointe work, she can apply these techniques to a full range of vocabulary. Many steps from barre work through allegro can be elevated to be performed en pointe, as for example battement glissé or pas de bourrée. In each case, the basic step must be solidly mastered before it is embellished or incorporated into enchaînements.

The specific movements described in this chapter are included because they require explanation beyond the basics. The technique of jumping en pointe, for example, embodies advanced technical principles. Although it builds from safe practices for relevés and basic allegro work, jumps en pointe require unique care and control. The bend at the knee and ankle must be limited and carefully timed to produce a controlled terre à terre spring. The knee, ankle, and foot must be precisely aligned to produce a secure push-off from the small base of support en pointe. And this precise placement must be retained on each balanced landing. Once mastered, however, this technique may be the crowning achievement of pointe work, adding sparkle and brilliance to female variations.

[1] For information on how to select and prepare shoes, see "Straight to the Pointe" by Moira McCormack, *dance gazette*, Issue 3 2001, pages 44-45.

COUPE FOUETTE RACCOURCI

A coupé action leading into a posé en pointe to 2nd position en l'air and ending with an inward whipping action of the working leg.

En face, left foot sur le cou-de-pied derrière en fondu; arms 3rd position right arm forward; eye focus over the right forearm:

Stepping strongly onto pointe, with a coupé action of the left leg, the right leg extends to 2nd position at 45 degrees. The right leg then executes an inward whipping action that finishes mid-calf height derrière as the left leg lowers en fondu.

The right arm moves to 2nd position with the outward action of the right leg, head to 1, and the left arm moves across to 3rd position on the inward action, with the eye focus over the left forearm.

This movement may be executed en tournant, with a 1/2-turn on the coupé and outward action of the leg.

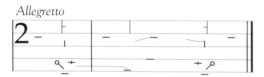

Allegretto

Coupé fouetté raccourci in 2/4 time

BALLOTTE DESSOUS AND DESSUS

Facing 6, left leg 4th position derrière en l'air at 90 degrees en fondu; arms 3rd position right arm forward; eye focus over the right forearm:

Ballotté dessous: from 4th position derrière, the right leg straightens to rise en pointe as the left leg makes an enveloppé action to retiré derrière and the trunk adjusts to the upright position. At the same time, the right arm opens toward 2nd position as the left arm moves toward 1st position and the head turns toward 1. The left leg then closes to 5th position derrière en pointes and the right leg is immediately drawn up through retiré devant to execute a développé devant finishing en fondu. The upper body inclines slightly backward as the arms arrive in 3rd position with the left arm forward and the head to 1 at the completion of the movement.

Ballotté dessus: from 4th position devant, the left leg straightens to rise en pointe as the right leg makes an enveloppé action to retiré devant and the trunk adjusts to the upright position. At the same time, the left arm opens toward 2nd position as the right arm moves toward 1st position. The right leg then closes to 5th position devant en pointes and the left leg is immediately drawn up through retiré derrière to execute a développé derrière finishing en fondu. The upper body inclines slightly forward as the arms arrive in 3rd position with the right arm forward and the eye focus over the right forearm at the completion of the movement.

The adjustment of the body weight necessary to achieve the rocking action requires balance over the supporting leg and control from a strong centre. A strong pull up from the back of the thigh assists the lift onto pointe. The counterforce downwards through the taut leg and foot ensures greater control through the smaller base of support.

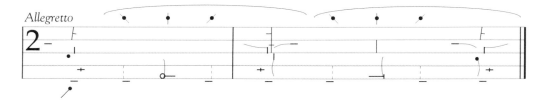

Ballotté dessous and dessus in 2/4 time

SISSONNE FERMEE RELEVEE

A travelled relevé from two feet which make a scissor-like action before closing.

SISSONNE FERMEE RELEVEE DE COTE DESSUS

En face, 5th position right foot derrière; bras bas:

From a demi-plié, there is a strong push-off both feet. With the relevé action, the weight is immediately transferred onto pointe travelling to the left, with the left leg fully stretched under the body and the right leg extended to 2nd position at 45 degrees. Both feet then close simultaneously into 5th position en demi-plié, right leg devant.

Sissonne fermée relevée may also be taken de côté dessous, devant, derrière, and en avant and en arrière.

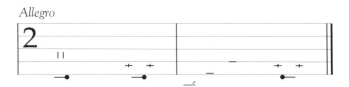

Sissonne fermée relevée de côté dessus in 2/4 time

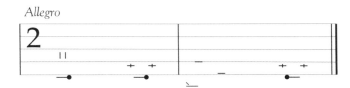

Sissonne fermée relevée de côté dessous in 2/4 time

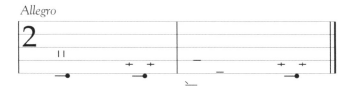

Sissonne fermée relevée de côté devant in 2/4 time

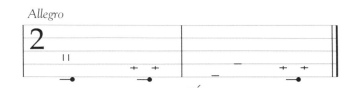

Sissonne fermée relevée de côté derrière in 2/4 time

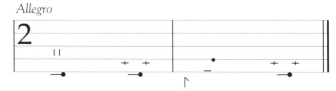

Sissonne fermée relevée en avant in 2/4 time

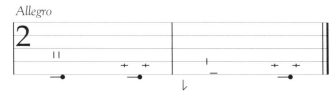

Sissonne fermée relevée en arrière in 2/4 time

SISSONNE OUVERTE RELEVEE DE COTE

En face, 5th position right foot devant; bras bas:

From a demi-plié, there is a strong push-off both feet. With the relevé action, the weight is immediately transferred onto pointe travelling sideways toward the back foot, with the left leg fully stretched under the body and the right leg extended to 2nd position at 45 degrees. The position of the raised leg is sustained as the supporting leg lowers en fondu.

Sissonne ouverte relevée may be taken de côté travelling sideways toward the front foot, and also en avant and en arrière.

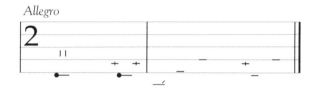

Sissonne ouverte relevée de côté travelling toward the back foot in 2/4 time

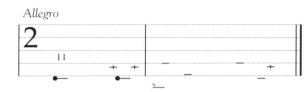

Sissonne ouverte relevée de côté travelling toward the front foot in 2/4 time

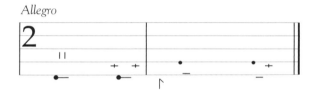

Sissonne ouverte relevée en avant in 2/4 time

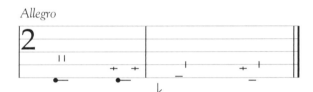

Sissonne ouverte relevée en arrière in 2/4 time

EMBOITE

A series of quick, precise transferences of weight taken under the body line, with the legs passing one in front of the other in a sideways action.

En face, 5th position en pointes, right foot derrière; arms demi-seconde:

From 5th position en pointes, the right foot is released to 2nd position at glissé height. It passes into 5th position devant and the left leg is immediately released to 2nd position at glissé height, ready for the next weight transference. The movement remains en pointe throughout.

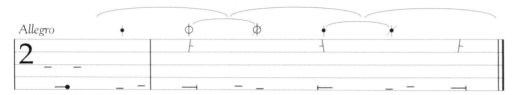

Emboîté in 2/4 time

SAUTE EN POINTES

A small, low jump taking off from and landing en pointes.

SAUTE EN POINTES IN 5TH POSITION

En face, 5th position en pointes, right foot devant; bras bas:

From a small demi-plié with the knees and ankles slightly flexed, the spring is just high enough to allow the knees and ankles to stretch before landing en pointes in the small demi-plié position.

In order to bear the weight safely through the pointes, the flexion of the knees and ankles should not be over-emphasised.

Sautés may also be taken on one leg en pointe, with the same action.

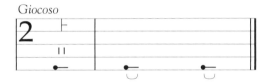

Sauté en pointes in 5th position in 2/4 time